D1429930

Elite • 220

European Counter-Terrorist Units

1972–2017

LEIGH NEVILLE

ILLUSTRATED BY ADAM HOOK
Series editor Martin Windrow

Osprey Publishing
c/o Bloomsbury Publishing Plc
PO Box 883, Oxford, OX1 9PL, UK
Or:
c/o Bloomsbury Publishing Inc
1385 Broadway, 5th Floor, New York, NY 10018, USA
E-mail: info@ospreypublishing.com

www.ospreypublishing.com

OSPREY is a trademark of Osprey Publishing Ltd, a division of Bloomsbury
Publishing Plc.

First published in Great Britain in 2017

© 2017 Osprey Publishing Ltd.

All rights reserved. No part of this publication may be used or reproduced
in any form, without prior written permission, except in the case of brief
quotations embodied in critical articles or reviews. Enquiries should be
addressed to the Publishers.

A CIP catalogue record for this book is available from the British Library

ISBN: PB: 978 1 4728 2527 8
         ePub: 978 1 4728 2528 5
         ePDF: 978 1 4728 2529 2
         XML: 978 1 4728 2530 8

17 18 19 20 21   10 9 8 7 6 5 4 3 2 1

Editor: Martin Windrow
Index by Fionbar Lyons
Typeset in Sabon and Myriad Pro

Page layouts by PDQ Digital Media Solutions, Bungay, UK
Printed in China through World Print Ltd

ARTIST'S NOTE

Readers may care to note that the original paintings from which the colour
plates in this book were prepared are available for private sale. All
reproduction copyright whatsoever is retained by the Publisher. All
enquiries should be addressed to:

Scorpio,158 Mill Road, Hailsham, East Sussex BN27 2SH, UK
scorpiopaintings@btinternet.com

The Publishers regret that they can enter into no correspondence upon
this matter.

Osprey Publishing supports the Woodland Trust, the UK's leading woodland
conservation charity. Between 2014 and 2018 our donations are being
spent on their Centenary Woods project in the UK.

To find out more about our authors and books,
visit **www.ospreypublishing.com**. Here you will find extracts, author
interviews, details of forthcoming events, and the option to sign up for
our newsletter.

DEDICATION

To all past and present members of the intervention teams, particularly to
those who have been wounded in the line of duty, or who have made the
ultimate sacrifice in the fight against terror.

ACKNOWLEDGEMENTS

Thanks to my wife Jodi, my editor Martin Windrow, and to the intervention
teams themselves. A particular thank you to GIGN, GSG9, RAID, NOCS, EKO
Cobra and Argus; and to Dom Andre at *Flashbang Magazine* for his gracious
support.

AUTHOR'S NOTE

Every unit featured in this book arguably deserves a book of its own. The
author has concentrated on the older and larger units within the European
counter-terrorist (CT) community, while attempting to provide at least
some information on as many of the smaller and lesser-known units as
possible. As can be imagined, this was a delicate balancing act within the
constraints of the book's format. Hopefully this book may enjoy enough
success to justify further volumes that will allow fuller treatment.

In a similar vein, readers may question why certain units with CT
responsibilities are not included or are covered in lesser detail. Again, the
format has obliged me to make the hard decision to focus on units that
have CT as their *primary or sole mission*. The book also focuses primarily on
Western European units because of limited access to research sources in
other languages. Again, hopefully we can cover these units in more detail
in a future volume. Readers will also note that we have used the European
term 'intervention unit' to differentiate between those conducting actual
tactical operations against terrorists, and those conducting investigations
of terrorist suspects (although these too are often referred to as the
'counter-terrorist' or 'anti-terrorist' squad or branch).

Finally, an apology for the inevitably heavy use of abbreviations and
acronyms. Nearly all of the units featured refer to themselves by their initial
letters, and this is reflected in the text. Likewise many of their weapons,
equipment and techniques are known by abbreviations. We have explained
the definition of each at its first appearance in the text, but readers are also
directed to the glossary at the back of the book.

CONTENTS

EUROPEAN COUNTER-TERRORIST UNITS 1972–2017

THE LESSON OF MUNICH

On 5 September 1972, Palestinian Black September terrorists broke into the quarters of the Israeli team at the Munich Olympic Village and took 11 hostages, two of whom were subsequently murdered. Negotiations saw the terrorists demand the release of a large number of Palestinian terrorists held in Israeli jails, along with the two founders of the Red Army Faction (RAF), a German far-left radical group. Finally, they demanded a chartered flight to Cairo to spirit the terrorists away.

In 1972 no dedicated counter-terrorist intervention force existed in any European country. The Germans were caught completely unprepared for the Munich incident, and their response was amateurish at best. After repeated threats against the hostages, the German government informed the terrorists that their demands would be met; they would be flown by helicopter to Furstenfeldbruck airport, where they would board a Lufthansa aircraft that would take them to Cairo. In fact, the German police planned to neutralize the terrorists at Furstenfeldbruck. A small team of police officers, disguised in Lufthansa crew uniforms, were tasked with killing or capturing the terrorists when they boarded the aircraft. Any who escaped would be gunned down by a team of police marksmen on the perimeter. At literally the last minute, the disguised officers decided amongst themselves that the operation was too risky, and they stood down. The intervention was left instead to a five-man team of marksmen, who were now to ambush the terrorists as they arrived at the airport.

The terrorists and their hostages were transported to Furstenfeldbruck by military helicopter, one of which landed barely 50 metres from the marksmen. Illustrating the appalling quality of police intelligence, the marksmen were surprised when eight terrorists, not the five that they had planned for, disembarked. As the terrorists left the helicopters to approach the getaway plane the order was given to open fire. The marksmen, none of whom were trained snipers, missed their targets and triggered a protracted and bloody firefight, which resulted in the deaths of all of the hostages, one policeman, and five of the eight terrorists. In the confusion two of the police marksmen were even shot by fellow officers. The operation was an unmitigated disaster.

The German authorities were roundly criticized for their handling of the operation. To add insult to injury, Germany

An iconic 1979 recruiting poster for West Germany's Border Police Group 9. It shows an abseiling officer wearing the earlier Bundeswehr paratrooper's helmet (later replaced with the famous TIG design with a camouflage cover) and armed with an MP5A2 fitted with two straight magazines fixed together for rapid reloading. He also carries a Smith & Wesson .357 revolver on a belt with extra cartridge loops. (Photo Kucharz/ullstein bild via Getty Images)

A late-1970s image of Col Ulrich Wegener, commander of GSG9 (left), wearing the Federal Border Police green beret, and a five-man Sonder-Einsatztrupp (SET, 'special action squad') of his unit; see Plate A1. The officers wear British-made Bristol body armour, and carry (from left to right:) a 12-gauge HK502 shotgun; a 9mm MP5A2 SMG; an MP5SD3 sound-suppressed SMG fitted with an early Hensoldt Aiming Point illuminator; and a 40mm HK69 grenade launcher. (Photo Kucharz/ullstein bild via Getty Images)

A classic image of a 22 SAS Special Projects team from the early 1980s photographed during a train assault exercise; compare with Plate A2. Note the black Bristol armour with pouches for ceramic trauma plates (similar to the green-coloured version used by GSG9); the large Maglite flashlights mounted over the receivers of their MP5s; and the extended 20-round magazines in the 9mm Browning High Power pistols carried in drop holsters. (Photographer unknown; private collection)

released the surviving Black September terrorists the following month after a Lufthansa airliner on a flight from Damascus to Frankfurt was hijacked to gain leverage. The Federal Ministry of the Interior immediately and quietly took steps to ensure that Germany would have an effective CT response in future. This initiative led directly to the formation of the first dedicated intervention unit within Europe: the famous Grenzschutzgruppe 9 or GSG9 of the Federal Border Police. Its first commander, Col (now Gen) Ulrich 'Ricky' Wegener, was adamant: 'We could not afford another Munich.' Following Germany's lead, many European governments began to establish their own intervention teams.

Amongst the first were the French, with the equally famous Groupe d'Intervention de la Gendarmerie Nationale (GIGN), and the British, who tasked the Army's 22 Special Air Service (SAS) Regt with developing a CT capability. While these early units were still being established international terrorism increased in both frequency and violence; this was spurred on by the rapid growth in global television coverage, meaning that terrorist demands could be heard by an ever growing audience. Equally, after Munich many European governments simply acceded to terrorist demands, paying ransoms or releasing prisoners. This policy of appeasement had a negative effect on the development and particularly the deployment of intervention units. Many governments were simply too frightened of the consequences of an operation going wrong, with hostages murdered in the glare of the world's media, to commit to deploying their fledgling CT units. Equally, they feared the public relations implications of even a successful intervention.

The late Capt Andrew Massey of the British SAS, architect of the first SAS CT efforts, measured the mood when he noted in a 1972 report: 'use of shock tactics [by the SAS to resolve a terrorist incident] is certain to produce violent scenes abhorrent to the public eye, and likely to provoke unfavourable press reaction'. It would not be until after the Israeli operation at Entebbe in 1976, and GSG9's successful liberation of a hijacked Lufthansa flight in 1977, that European governments began to believe that tactical interventions against terrorists could work.

The enemy

Other than Palestinians, the terrorists of the 1970s and into the 1980s were predominantly far left or far right-wing organizations that grew out of an international mood of student radicalism and nihilism; there were few if any 'jihadists' as we know them today. The terrorists of the time would often work together towards common goals. For instance, the Japanese Red Army (JRA) carried out a murderous attack at Israel's Lod airport in 1972 in support of imprisoned German Red Army Faction terrorists. Many groups were also financially sponsored by Warsaw Pact intelligence agencies. Favoured tactics included airliner hijackings, and the kidnap and often murder of prominent political or business figures. Terrorist hijackings would see aircraft flown to a sympathetic state such as Libya, where the terrorists were given active support in terms of both security and supplies, far beyond the striking range of any European CT unit. Hostage-takings in embassies and consulates also increased in popularity.

The successful counter-operations at Entebbe in July 1976 and Mogadishu in October 1977 began to influence a slow but steady decrease in aircraft hijackings. Successful hostage rescues such as the British SAS operation at the Iranian Embassy in London in May 1980 also had a direct impact on the incidence of terrorist seizures of diplomatic premises.

A

GERMANY, BRITAIN & ITALY, 1980s
(1) German GSG9, 1980s
This officer is typical of the unit's appearance in the early to mid-1980s. His body armour is a British Bristol design in olive green, originally developed for the SAS, while his helmet is the distinctive PSH-77 titanium TIG with a splinter-pattern cover. He wears early Adidas GSG9 boots, custom-made for the unit. He carries the 9mm Heckler & Koch MP5A2 sub-machine gun with fixed stock; the straight magazine was later replaced with the familiar curved pattern to improve reliability with hollowpoint ammunition. The Hensoldt Aiming Point projector mounted above the receiver on proprietary H&K claw mounts is often misidentified as a visible laser, but is in fact a white light with projected reticle. His sidearm is the 9mm Heckler & Koch P7 PSP 'squeeze-cocker'.
(1a) GSG9 right breast badge
(2) British 22 SAS Pagoda Team, 1980
He wears an issue S6 respirator and a Royal Navy anti-flash hood, with black coveralls. Those worn at the time of the Iranian Embassy siege were reportedly standard British Army tank crew issue dyed black to increase the intimidation factor. He wears black Bristol body armour with trauma-plate inserts, under a custom-made suede 'ops waistcoat'; this holds ammunition and flashbang grenades, a Storno push-

to-talk (PTT) button attached to a Pye PF1 Pocketfone 70 series radio carried in a pouch on the side of his belt rig, and a Royal Air Force gravity knife (which some troopers wore on the upper right sleeve). His primary weapon is the MP5A3 SMG, with collapsible stock and a large Maglite flashlight mounted over the receiver; only about half the MP5s used during Operation 'Nimrod' had this attachment, and an early version of the Streamlight purpose-designed weapon light was also used. His sidearm in the distinctive drop holster is the 9mm L9A1 Browning High Power with 20-round extended magazine.
(3) Italian NOCS, late 1980s
Many police teams, such as the Nucleo Operativo Centrale di Sicurezza, favoured blue rather than black coveralls. This officer sports an arc-shaped national flag tab on his right shoulder, and on his left both a 'POLIZIA' title and the NOCS unit patch (of which a later version incorporates the unit's acronym – see below). This early assault vest features a right shoulder pad, chest loops for 12-gauge shotgun shells, and integral magazine pouches. His weapon is the 7.62mm Heckler & Koch PSG-1, widely regarded to this day as one of the most accurate semi-automatic sniper rifles ever built, and employed at times by the SAS, GSG9 and the Spanish GEO.
(3a) NOCS sleeve patch

3

1

2

3a

SICUT NOX SILENTES

N.O.C.S.

1a

THE CHANGING FACE OF TERRORISM

Terrorism in Europe can be divided into three distinct phases. The 1970s–80s saw political extremists and Palestinian groups conducting kidnappings, hijackings and bombings in a concerted effort against Western governments and Israel. In the 1990s–2000s the nature of terrorism changed as the majority of European groups withered, thanks to both concerted police work and attempts at a political resolution to the Palestinian problem. Instead, since the world-changing events of 11 September 2001 in New York and Washington, followed by terrorist bombings in Madrid and London, recent decades have been haunted by the nihilist atrocities of al Qaeda and other Salafist (Sunni Muslim extremist) groups, characterized by a willingness to use human suicide-bombers. The US-led invasions of Afghanistan and Iraq subsequently attracted thousands of recruits to the jihadist movement, spawning today's chaotic environment of 'lone wolf' and mass casualty attacks sponsored or inspired by Daesh (the self-proclaimed 'Islamic State' or 'caliphate' in the Middle East).

Today's intervention units must train increasingly for what is known as the Marauding Terrorist Firearms Attack (MTFA): dynamic incidents akin to the Mumbai, Nairobi and Paris attacks, where multiple terrorists armed with automatic weapons, and probably suicide-bomb vests, attack soft public targets such as hotels, shopping malls, and places and events that attract large crowds of civilians. The perpetrators are no longer interested in ransoms or political demands: they stage these attacks with the sole intent of causing mass civilian casualties, which are seen as an end in themselves.

Complicating the intervention response is the fact that incidents may occur at multiple locations (such as the November 2015 Paris attacks), or form a chain of linked incidents (such as the *Charlie Hebdo* massacre and related attacks of January 2015). Previously, terrorists would often commit a single act and then either stay at the location in siege mode, taking hostages, or attempt to evade capture in order to fight another day. A senior German GSG9 officer explained this change: 'The terrorists of the self-proclaimed Islamic State act very decisively. So, as a special unit, we have to react even more decisively, even more directly and even more quickly. [Previously] we had time to prepare ourselves, and could gather intelligence about the perpetrators – perhaps even [conduct] a dress rehearsal on a replica [of the location]. But we do not have all these possibilities in an attack like Nice, Paris or Brussels. We must immediately go to the place of the attack, so as to move our units in and stop the terrorists as soon as possible.'[1]

A former commander of the Belgian DSU intervention unit agreed: 'When I started [at DSU] back in 1989 we were living in a different age. There were around 20 large interventions every year. Most of these situations you could end by negotiations. If suspects needed to be neutralized we used, if possible, less [than] lethal weapons. It goes without saying that we have to deal with totally different people

Intervention in three dimensions: French GIGN operators conduct a 2009 exercise against a 'hijacked' tourist bus. Note the Chevrolet SWATEC assault trucks fitted with the Height Adjustable Rescue System (HARAS), and the hovering Puma helicopter, which carries an aerial sniper team. (Photo Bertrand Guay/AFP/Getty Images)

1 For sources of quotations, see notes on page 61 after the Bibliography.

[today] than in the past.' Often the terrorists themselves want martyrdom: 'These are the guys who are clearly disappointed when we capture them alive. They would rather have died as "martyrs" in a rattling firefight with police. If we prevent that from happening by arresting them alive, they see it as a tremendous dishonour. A terrorist once explicitly asked us to kill him. When we told him we wouldn't, we could see the disappointment on his face.

'When terrorists immediately open fire at the police or are able to escape and run into the streets there is no room for negotiation, of course. Then we have to act immediately – there are no other options. We have to avoid at all costs that they harm innocent civilians. From experience, we know some terrorists wear an explosive belt which they do not hesitate to use. Others open fire on everything that moves with fully-automatic rifles.' [2] Many of today's terrorists have experienced some form of combat in Syria or Yemen, for example, or at least may have received rudimentary paramilitary training. They are also likely to be carrying AK-series assault rifles and to have access to fragmentation grenades, or even heavier weapons such as RPGs obtained through the Balkans black market. They may be wearing body armour as well as suicide-bomb vests. 'They know what it's like to be fired upon. During normal interventions we are able to disorient suspects with non-lethal grenades, [but such] flashbangs don't make an impression on these terrorists. Normal people are terrified when we throw these grenades; these terrorists don't even flinch,' explained the Belgian officer.

Terrorists in the 21st century are transnational, crossing borders with ease using stolen or doctored passports, or concealing themselves in the flow of refugees arriving in Europe from war-torn Syria. The November 2015 Paris attackers criss-crossed Europe and operated from a forward base in Belgium. 'There are scenarios that cannot be met with purely national resources,

GIGN officers during an exercise to retake a Metro train in 2016. They carry a mix of 5.56mm HK416 and 7.62mm HK417 assault rifles; the coloured chemlights looped to the groin armour (centre) are for marking cleared areas or suspect devices. The officer on the right appears to wear part of an EOD 'bomb suit', suggesting that he may be from the GIGN's Operational Support Force. (Photo Miguel Medina/AFP/Getty Images)

GIGN assault element, complete with a combat assault dog, standing by during the Dammartin-en-Goële siege of the CTD print works on 9 January 2015. (Photo © Gendarmerie Nationale/F. Balsamo)

because today we are dealing mainly with a cross-national phenomenon of crime. Whether terrorism or organized crime, everything becomes more international. Against this background, it is of particular importance that we strengthen our cooperation with our counterparts on an international level.'

The situation seems unlikely to improve, at least while Daesh and al Qaeda maintain the clarion call of their death-cult. The nature of the threat is evolving to include tactics more commonly seen on the streets of Baghdad

B **AUSTRIA, SPAIN & FRANCE, 1990s-2001**

(1) Austrian GEK/EKO Cobra, late 1990s

This Einsatzkommando Cobra operator wears a distinctive Ulbrichts AM-95 ballistic helmet with visor and *Flecktarn* camouflage-pattern cover. The bulges at the side are built-in compartments for combined ear-protection/communications headsets such as those manufactured by Peltor. On his left sleeve are a large Austrian flag tab above a subdued-colour EKO patch. He is armed with the 5.56mm Steyr assault rifle, and a 9mm Glock 17 sidearm with Streamlight mount.

Ballistic visors are a distinctly European feature which can probably be traced to their early use by GSG9 and GIGN. They can be lifted up and out of the way when not needed, and are rated to defeat 9mm pistol rounds and shotgun pellets and to protect against grenade and IED fragments. Most models incorporate an outer layer that is designed to shatter when struck, leaving an inner layer to protect the face. Disadvantages include fogging and reduced peripheral vision. Some teams, notably NOCS, have even used full-face ballistic masks that resemble motocross riders' equipment.

(1a) Full-colour EKO Cobra sleeve patch

(2) Spanish GEO, c. 2001

This sniper from the Grupo Especial de Operaciones displays a (relatively) subdued GEO eagle-and-snake patch on his right shoulder and a full-colour National Police patch on his left. His weapon is the unusual DSR-1 sniper rifle chambered for the 7.62mm NATO round. Although a traditional bolt-action

weapon, it is built with a free-floating barrel for maximum accuracy, while the 'bullpup' design maintains the shortest possible overall length. The DSR-1 has also been adopted by GSG9 and several German SEKs. Lying in the foreground is a 40mm HK69A1 standalone grenade launcher, used to deliver CS gas and chemical irritant Ferret rounds.

(3) French GIGN, 1994

This officer from the Groupe d'Intervention de la Gendarmerie Nationale is dressed and equipped as one of the primary assaulters on to Air France Flight 8969 (see Plate E). He wears the MSA Gallet assault helmet with yellow-tinted ballistic glass visor, blue Nomex coveralls, and Adidas GSG9 boots. His visible weapon is the distinctive .357 Magnum Manurhin MR73 Gendarmerie revolver, although the operators also carried the 9mm Glock 19.

The MR73 plays an important role within GIGN, and has also been issued to RAID and EKO Cobra. Since its inception GIGN have issued each officer with two – one short-barrelled, and one with a 6in barrel and drilled to accept optics (they even have a 10in-barrel version available, with scope and bipod). The MR73 is used in a unique confidence-building ritual for all recruits who pass their initial 12 months with the unit: they are required to fire it at a clay pigeon ('skeet') secured to the chest of another operator's body armour, to demonstrate that the trauma plate will stop the round.

(3a) Full-colour GIGN left sleeve patch. There is a more recent subdued version in shades of grey.

1

3a

3

1a

2

or Kabul, such as suicide car-bombings, and 'lone wolf' attacks that require little training or logistic support, such as the deliberate ramming of civilian crowds with hijacked trucks – as seen in the 2016 incidents in Nice and Berlin. As the terrorist Amedy Coulibaly prophetically declared before his death at the hands of the French RAID intervention unit: 'There will be many more like me; many more will come.'

INTERVENTION TACTICS & TECHNIQUES

As readers will appreciate, there is much which cannot and should not be published in terms of intervention tactics, lest it provide an advantage for a future terrorist. Some generic tactics can be discussed, however, as they are already disseminated in the public domain. Here we will examine what a typical intervention against a terrorist 'stronghold' might entail.

Once the intervention unit arrives at the scene, they will establish an inner cordon around the target location, and position sniper teams to provide both overwatch and real-time intelligence on terrorist movements through their high-powered optics. Along with information from the sniper teams, units will deploy a number of tools to gather information on the location of both terrorists and hostages. Many teams employ video cameras mounted on extendable poles that allow operators to peer into a window or doorway, with streaming video beamed back to the command post. Units may also employ sophisticated devices such as the L3 Range-R that uses radar pulses to detect human beings on the other side of a wall or door. The system categorizes these radar returns as either 'movers' or 'breathers', and shows their approximate locations on a screen. More traditional 'bugs' may also be emplaced.

Increasingly, micro-UAVs (unmanned aerial vehicles, better known as 'drones') are being deployed, fitted with thermal cameras to pick up heat signatures from terrorists and hostages alike. As technology advances, these

An Italian NOCS assault team preparing to conduct a forced-entry exercise provide an excellent illustration of 'stacking'. Beside the shield-carrier (right background), the second man is armed with a breaching shotgun. The fifth man has a manual battering-ram in case the attempt at a ballistic breach fails. While the team prepare to deploy a pair of combat assault dogs, the pistol-armed rear guard watches their flanks. (Photo courtesy NOCS)

UAVs are steadily decreasing in size and increasing in capability, with the latest versions also capable of capturing audio. Wheeled or tracked UGVs (unmanned ground vehicles or 'droids'), originally developed from Explosive Ordnance Disposal (EOD) equipment and mounting a range of sensors, are also increasingly employed.

After a decision has been taken to assault the location, the intervention unit will often approach in multiple 'stacks' of four to five operators, each with a lead scout with ballistic shield, an operator covering him or her with a sub-machine gun or carbine, a third or fourth operator covering the flanks, and finally the rear guard providing security at the tail end (see Plate C).

Ballistic shields are widely employed by European teams. These range from folding, flexible shields that can also act as ballistic blankets, to designs featuring built-in white light strobes to disorientate terrorists during an entry, or low-light video cameras enabling the operator to view the scene on a tablet-sized screen mounted on the reverse of the shield. Heavy shields proofed against the 7.62x39mm round fired from the AK-47, and referred to as 'bunkers', are often used to provide portable cover as the assault team approach their entry point. The Ramses modular wheeled shield is one famous example used at the 2015 Bataclan siege in Paris, although versions were used by the firearms unit of London's Metropolitan Police as far back as 1976 to facilitate the safe recovery of casualties under fire.

The assault force might also include canines and their handlers, including specialist combat assault dogs (CADs) and explosive-detection dogs (EDDs). The use of dedicated and specially trained dogs was pioneered by the Belgian DSU using domestic Malinois (Belgian shepherds). Initially these dogs were used to assist in searching for explosives and later for people. Today's CADs

Austrian EKO Cobra operators travel to a target on the running boards of a Patriot 3 MARS intervention vehicle. The MARS system allows running boards to be raised or lowered to deliver assaulters at the correct height – for example, at window-level for a bus assault. These officers carry the 9mm B&T APC9 sub-machine gun. The second from the right, armed with a Glock pistol and wearing heavier armour, is probably the 'shield man' who will be the first through the door. (Photo courtesy BM.I/ Polizei)

An assault team from the Spanish GEO during an exercise in 2016. The vehicle is the so-called 'Spanish Humvee', the URO VAMTAC, fitted with a MARS adjustable ladder unit. The rifleman (centre) has a 7.62mm HK417 with a thermal day/night sight partnered with a telescopic optic; the assaulters carry MP5s with angled stocks to accommodate their visors. (Photo Pablo Cuadra/Getty Images)

Belgian DSU Intervention Unit operators with a Malinois (Belgian shepherd) dog, atop a modified Toyota Land Cruiser fitted with assault ladders. Their weapon is the distinctive 5.56mm Fabrique Nationale SCAR-L. (Photo courtesy Collectorofinsignia)

can enter a terrorist stronghold to conduct reconnaissance with a video camera strapped to their backs. Many of the European units have developed techniques and equipment to deploy their dogs whatever the location of the

C RAID ASSAULT TEAM; SAINT-DENIS, NOVEMBER 2015

This is an impression of the probable weapons and equipment carried by the RAID assaulters as they stacked up in the hallway leading to the terrorists' apartment at 8 rue de Courbillon in Saint-Denis, Paris, in the early hours of 18 November 2015.

(Left) Positioned just ahead of the team is an Austrian-made Ramses three-wheeled ballistic shield, comprising three folding panels; this type of shield, which will stop AK rounds, was employed during both the Bataclan Theatre and Saint-Denis operations.

(1) The lead officer covers the apartment door with his light-mounted Glock 17 pistol held at an angle over his ballistic shield, which is itself fitted with an LED light array. He wears a heavy MSA helmet with ballistic visor, though here without the neck protection worn by (2) and (3). Some photos of assault teams (e.g. see page 10) also show pouches for flashbang grenades fixed to the rear of body armour, allowing access for the next man in the 'stack'. On his left shoulder he displays the RAID patch. This is seen in both full-colour and subdued formats.

(1a) RAID sleeve patch

(2) Behind him, a handler controls his muzzled Belgian Malinois combat assault dog. He carries his Glock in a SERPA holster fixed to his armour plate carrier; visible next to the PTT radio button on his torso, note the extended pocket for a 33rd magazine, originally intended for the fully automatic Glock 18.

(3) The third operator watches the team's flanks; note on his right shoulder the 'FNIP' tab of the National Police Intervention Force, which the other officers would also wear. He is armed with a Russian 12-gauge Molot Vepr-12 semi-automatic shotgun fitted with an EOTech sight. Patterned after the Kalashnikov design, it has a side-folding stock and a 10rd detachable magazine. Note the handcuff case positioned between his Glock and the spare magazines on his drop-holster leg harness.

(4) Positioned here a little too close to the others for strict accuracy, this fourth officer is part of the containment team manning an inner perimeter. Since he will not form part of the entry team, he may hope to be adequately protected by the lighter Ops Core helmet. His weapon is the 7.62mm HK417 battle rifle, with a 6x magnified Trijicon EOTech optic.

target. Special harnesses allow dogs to be slung under an operator who must climb or fast-rope to reach a target. There are even rigs available for dogs to tandem-parachute with their handlers, including High Altitude High Opening (HAHO) jumps that require the dog to be equipped with its own oxygen.

A GIGN operator from their canine ('Cynophilic') cell explained: 'They are recruited to the same standards as the recruitment of men of the GIGN. Dogs must be calm, balanced... ability to remain silent is very important – [they] must sometimes stay for hours by the legs of their master without the slightest barking. They are selected between the ages of 6 and 18 months, then trained for about a year. Their career lasts until the age of 8 years. They are almost exclusively Malinois Belgian shepherds.'[3]

Assault vehicles

Intervention units may also employ specialist vehicles to enable them to reach a target. Typical of these is the Chevrolet SWATEC fitted with the HARAS or Height Adjustable Rescue Assault System, as used by GIGN (see Plate H). The HARAS system allows an entry team to be delivered right up to the passenger doors of commercial airliners, for instance, with an adjustable height of up to 8.65m (28.4ft) above the ground. The HARAS even features fold-down armoured floor panels that serve as ballistic shields.

In 2013 GIGN also purchased the Renault Sherpa 4x4 in its light APC variant, sometimes known as the 'French Hummer'. It does superficially resemble the famous American design, but can accommodate ten operators under armour, along with a HARAS mount and running boards to transport further officers on the outside. This vehicle had its debut at the Dammartin-en-Goële siege in 2015. The London Metropolitan Police's SCO19 have used the Ford F450-based Jenkel Guardian since 2002, replacing a number of armoured Land Rovers that had served the unit since 1979. The 7-tonne Jenkel (seen in the streets of London after the Westminster terror attack on 22 March 2017) is also fitted with ladders and extended running boards, and is heavily armoured in case a team need to approach a target location under

Austria's EKO Cobra conduct a dynamic breach into a simulated terrorist 'stronghold'. Under magnification, the MOE operator leading the team at the top of the left-hand ladder can be seen reaming broken window glass with a specialist tool, while his colleague covers him with a 5.56mm Steyr AUG; the third officer is armed with a 9mm APC9 sub-machine gun. (Photo courtesy BM.I/Polizei)

A pair of breachers from EKO Cobra, preparing to deploy a battering ram, wear covers in the distinctive German *Flecktarn* camouflage on their Ulbricht AM-95 ballistic helmets. Note the load-bearing vest worn over the body armour, and the modular armour attachments. (Photo courtesy BM.I/Polizei)

fire. GSG9 have a range of customized Land Rover Defenders that include rooftop platforms and adjustable running boards, designed to deposit an assault team at the correct height to break into the windows of a hijacked bus or coach.

Some units, including GSG9 and the SAS, have the luxury of their own dedicated helicopters, which can deploy assault teams via fast rope, or orbit the incident to provide aerial sniper overwatch. Both GIGN and GSG9 specialize in the use of a device known as the AirTEP or Airborne Tactical Extraction Platform manufactured by Capewell Aerial Systems (see Plate H). This is a collapsible platform constructed from Kevlar webbing that can be lowered from a helicopter and, once deployed to its 3m (9.8ft) diameter, can carry up to ten people. Both units employ the AirTEP for rapid extraction of hostages or wounded, but also practise using it to deploy assault teams into locations that are otherwise difficult to access.

Breaching

However the approach is made, once the team arrives at the identified breach point they will stack up on the door, with a specially trained breacher moving into position to make the forced entry using a range of Method of Entry (MOE) tools and techniques. These may be mechanical, explosive, thermal or ballistic.

Mechanical breaching may involve the use of pneumatic or hydraulic units like the Libervit Door Raider, which can open even reinforced doors almost silently and in seconds. Some of the more advanced models even include remote control operation, thus giving protection in case of explosive booby-traps, and allowing the insertion of a CAD or UGV to provide live video reconnaissance before the assault team enters. At the opposite end of the mechanical spectrum is a range of more conventional tools, from traditional hand-held battering rams like the Enforcer to the crowbar-like Halligan Tool, which uses manual pressure to bust open doors. Even sledgehammers are employed, although these are often carried as a secondary, fall-back tool. Breaking windows is accomplished with specialist tools that resemble ice axes, designed to defeat all types of glass and allow the operator to rake the remaining glass from the window frame. Some units, such as Austria's EKO Cobra, use a specially designed shovel with embedded glass-breaking spikes for this task. So-called 'bang poles' incorporate a glass-breaking tool and a flashbang grenade mount on the end of a telescoping aluminium pole; the operator uses the glass-breaker to smash in a window before deploying the flashbang into the entry point.

The Explosive Method of Entry (EMOE) is conducted using frame charges of explosives positioned to either destroy a door or blow a hole through a wall. EMOE allows an intervention team to conduct an entry through virtually any surface, including the walls, ceiling, or even up through the floor of a target location. An alternative to the frame charge is the door-breaching rifle grenade, such as the Israeli Simon design, which allows a door to be explosively breached from a safe distance. Other specialist devices allow frame charges to be attached to extendable poles, in a variant of the bang pole that can be positioned to destroy upper-storey doors or windows.

Thermal entry, unsurprisingly, involves the use of a thermal lance or similar oxyacetylene device to cut through a metal door. These devices are rarely used except for assaults where EMOE cannot be employed for safety reasons, or during Maritime Counter-Terrorist (MCT) missions where any explosion could be catastrophic.

Finally, ballistic breaching involves the use of a specially designed 12-gauge shotgun round known generically as the Hatton after the original manufacturer. These breaching rounds are made from powdered metal encased in wax, which dissipates and expends all of its energy in the lock or hinge, making them relatively safe to use with hostages nearby. They have also been found to be excellent for quickly deflating vehicle tyres. Doors can, of course, also be breached with standard buckshot shotgun rounds, or (as the SAS did during Operation 'Nimrod' in 1980) by firing short bursts from sub-machine guns, although these methods drastically increase the risk of harm to innocents; the Hatton and similar rounds are a far safer option. SCO19 even carry a 12-gauge Benelli M3 shotgun which they term the 'Hatton gun', as its sole function is to destroy locks, hinges and tyres using these specialist cartridges.

The MOE operator of a French RAID assault team prepares to breach a door. MOE packs carry a range of breaching tools, from Halligan Tools and bolt-cutters to sledgehammers, such as the model produced by Blackhawk Industries. (Photo courtesy RAID/DGPN-SICOP)

The assault

Once the breach has been achieved, the assault team will enter the objective while deploying a range of distraction devices to gain even a momentary advantage. These devices will typically include CS gas (often delivered by 40mm or 12-gauge Ferret rounds, which can penetrate windows and walls), capsicum spray or similar irritants, along with the 'stun' grenade, better known as the 'flashbang'. Today's flashbangs are 'multi-bang' devices, typically detonating up to eight or nine times in succession to increase the discomfort, blindness and deafness of the terrorists as the team enters the location.

Operators will clear the target location by 'slicing the pie' – dividing each room up into sectors that are covered by one operator as the team enter a room immediately after their flashbangs. Terrorists encountered will be engaged unless they immediately and visibly surrender. Hostages are bypassed until all of the terrorists are accounted for, when follow-on teams move them swiftly from the location to what is termed a hostage reception area, where their identities will be confirmed and any necessary first aid given. As rooms are cleared, infra-red or colour-coded 'chemlights' or 'glow sticks' are dropped by the operators to signal that an area has been cleared. Other colours are used to mark suspected Improvised Explosive Devices (IEDs) or booby-traps. Many units have their own integrated Explosive Ordnance Disposal operator attached to the team to render safe any devices or suicide-bomb vests that may be encountered.

Tailoring tactics to locations

All such tactics of course become exponentially more difficult to employ depending upon the type or location of the target. Hostage rescues against ships underway or against off-shore oil or gas platforms are among the trickiest to coordinate, and will see a mixture of insertion methods. Operators from specialist dive teams may covertly affix assault ladders, or scale the hull to conduct a reconnaissance prior to the assault. The assault itself will see teams arriving by small high-speed boats, and by helicopter with assaulters fast-roping to the deck. Overhead, heliborne snipers will cover the insertion of the intervention unit.

Dramatic image of Italian NOCS assaulters approaching a 'hijacked' aircraft by means of the HARAS system. In the background, others are deploying from unmarked vans, probably to man the inner cordon and handle released hostages, and a further assault team is moving up on mobile airstairs. (Photo courtesy NOCS)

During exercises in 2009, GIGN assaulters prepare to breach and storm a hijacked airliner, while a second assault element await their turn below the fuselage. The primary assaulters are all armed with Glock pistols, due to the confined space on board an aircraft. (Photo Alain Jocard/AFP/Getty Images)

Trains, aircraft and buses also provide their own challenges. Again, without going into operational specifics, the intervention units train for such so-called 'tubular' or 'linear' assaults in order to achieve maximum speed and surprise, overwhelming the terrorists before they can harm hostages or trigger a device. Assaults on buses see operators deploying via the custom-made intervention vehicles described above, allowing them to quickly breach the glass and lob in distraction devices. Other operators are assigned as designated shooters, to engage and neutralize the terrorists while their colleagues conduct the entry and rescue the hostages.

Aircraft require their own set of tactics. The GSG9 liberation of Lufthansa Flight 181 at Mogadishu in 1977 and the GIGN assault on the hijacked Air France Flight 8969 at Marseille in 1994 both remain excellent examples of

NOCS storming a hijacked train during a 'tubular assault' exercise. The operators wear visored MSA Gallet helmets; their weapons are a mix of Aimpoint-fitted MP5s and 9mm Beretta PX4 Storm pistols fitted with light mounts. This unit is one of the few to issue pistols other than Glocks, and has a history of using domestically produced weapons from Beretta and Franchi. (Photo courtesy NOCS)

RAID conducting a bus assault exercise in Paris, 2014. The rear windows have been smashed in with specialist tools, to allow flashbangs to be deployed as the entry team boards via the forward door. (Photo Thomas Samson/AFP/Getty Images)

such tactics, and are discussed later in this book. Both used diversions to ensure the maximum number of terrorists were located in the cabin when the assault was launched, in the French case allowing snipers to engage the gunmen. Both also saw the intervention units conduct multiple breaches, ensuring that the aircraft could be flooded with operators as quickly as possible to minimize the possibility of the terrorists harming the hostages.

Modern tactics are, naturally, far more advanced, but still rely on the concepts of speed, aggression and surprise to overwhelm the terrorists. Many of the training and technological advances over the past 40 years have combined to vastly reduce the time it takes to breach a terrorist strongpoint, engage the terrorists and secure the hostages. Indeed, intervention units train to secure most commercial airliners within a phenomenal 6 seconds after they have entered the aircraft.

Intervention team training

Not surprisingly, all intervention units have roughly similar requirements in terms of recruiting standards. Typically, they are looking for personnel who are in their mid-30s or younger; have some experience within the parent military or police organization (a minimum of two to three years is common); have a clean disciplinary record; and can pass both tests of fitness standards and psychological assessments conducted by unit psychologists. After this initial assessment, recruits are then often subjected to a gruelling selection course, many of which are based on the notorious SAS model.

Once accepted for training, the recruit may undergo anything from three months to a year or more before they are offered a spot on the team. Italy's GIS requires a five-month basic qualification course in close-quarter battle, marksmanship, high-speed driving, close protection, unarmed combat and first aid, before the recruit progresses to a six-month specialist course in techniques such as combat diving, sniping, reconnaissance and surveillance, or specialist parachuting. Germany's GSG9 maintains a ten-month training course before an officer is even posted to one of the unit's three Combat Units to commence specialist training.

INTERVENTION UNIT PROFILES

The following are arranged in alphabetical order by nation.

Austria

Einsatzkommando (EKO) Cobra is under the command of the Austrian Ministry of the Interior's Directorate of Special Units, although it recruits from across the Austrian Federal Police. The unit was founded in 1978 as the Gendarmerieeinsatzkommando or GEK Cobra before changing their name to EKO Cobra in 2002. GEK Cobra was developed from an earlier protective security unit established in 1973 to guard Jewish immigrants from the Soviet Union against Palestinian terrorism. This Gendarmeriekommando (GK) Bad Vöslau was first deployed operationally in September of that year, when Palestinian terrorists seized a train carrying Soviet Jews. Although the release of the hostages was peacefully negotiated in a politically contentious move after the Austrian government ruled out an assault, it was an important first step in establishing what would become the world-class EKO Cobra.

Two years later, an OPEC (Organization of Petroleum Exporting Countries) meeting in Vienna was famously seized by the Venezuelan arch-terrorist 'Carlos the Jackal' (Illich Ramirez Sanchez) and members of the Popular Front for the Liberation of Palestine (PFLP). Although the GK was deployed, and a number of civilians had been murdered, again the Austrian government lacked the political resolve to authorize an armed intervention; instead a ransom was paid, and Carlos and the other terrorists walked free. By 1978, however, the wave of terrorism across Europe had forced a change of direction. Inspired by GSG9's success at Mogadishu and the Israeli Operation

D

BELGIUM, GERMANY & NETHERLANDS, since 2010

(1) Belgian DSU

This assaulter illustrates the kind of equipment worn since early in this decade by the Directorate of Special Units Intervention Unit – originally titled, under Belgium's bilingual system, the Escadron Special d'Intervention (ESI)/ Speciaal Interventie Eskadron (SIE), and in 2007–14 the CGSU. The DSU replaced their earlier black coveralls with olive green for assaulters, and recently with grey for snipers – both colours believed to be better suited to urban environments, and making friend/foe identification easier in situations where their opponents may well be dressed in black complete with balaclava hoods. The 5.56mm FN SCAR-L with EOTech optic has largely replaced the MP5 and P90 as the unit's primary weapon. His sidearm is the ubiquitous 9mm Glock 17 with a Glock TLR weapon light, carried in a drop holster.

(1a) DSU patch.

The original full-colour version of this subdued right sleeve patch had the central motif in black-and-white on a blue disc with a red rim, bearing the white titles 'ESCADRON SPECIAL D'INTERVENTION' round the upper arc and 'SPECIAAL INTERVENTIE ESKADRON' below. The central image of Diana the Huntress has remained unchanged during the various changes of designation.

(2) German GSG9/2 diver

Instead of the AM-95 this combat diver has a ProTec diving helmet, in a trade-off between protection and portability. He wears tactical dive boots, after removing the Force swim fins which hang from behind his belt. Like most similar intervention units, GSG9/2 use the German-manufactured Dräger LAR VI closed-circuit or 'rebreather' diving apparatus, to eliminate tell-tale air bubbles on the surface as they approach a target (here the mouthpiece hangs down over his chest tank). His weapons are the 5.56mm G36C equipped with a Trijicon ACOG optic and LLM01 laser light module, and a Glock 17 maritime variant known as the P9M, developed to drain water quickly and efficiently.

(3) Dutch UIM (BBE)

In 2006 the Bijzondere Bijstands Eenheid (BBE) of the Royal Netherlands Marine Corps was renamed the Unit Interventie Mariniers (UIM), but it is still widely known as the BBE. This assaulter demonstrates the current clothing and equipment. Worn over a Nomex hood, the MSA KFS V2 helmet has a ballistic visor and neck curtain. Over the blue Nomex coveralls he wears both knee pads and riot armour shin-protectors. The primary weapon is the 5.7mm FN P90, fitted with a sound suppressor, Aimpoint red-dot optic, and LLM01 laser module. His sidearm is the 9mm Glock 17 with Surefire light, worn in a tan drop holster.

(3a) Unit Interventie Mariniers sleeve patch.

Worn on the right arm; the abbreviations 'RNLMC/DSI' stand for Royal Netherlands Marine Corps and the CT joint coordinating command, Dienst Speciale Interventies. The RNLMC has long and close links with Britain's Royal Marines within NATO forces.

3

3a

RNLMC/DSI
UNIT INTERVENTIE MARINIERS

2

1

DSU
POLICE FÉDÉRALE POLITIE

'Thunderbolt' at Entebbe, the Austrian government transformed the GK into a direct-action counter-terrorist force, the Gendarmerieeinsatzkommando (GEK) Cobra. This new unit was developed with the close support of both GSG9 and the Israeli Sayaret Matkal.

Along with hostage rescue and the capture of both armed criminal and terrorist suspects, the new unit became responsible for providing an air marshal capability, and for the protection of government officials and embassies. GEK Cobra became known for its expertise in conducting opposed entries on virtually any transport system, be it a ship at sea, a train carriage or a bus. To facilitate this, specialist teams were trained in combat diving (Tauchschwimmers) and parachuting (Fallschirmspringers). The unit were also renowned climbers and adept at high-altitude rope work.

In October 1996, a four-man team from GEK Cobra were escorting extradited prisoners on board a Russian airliner when a Nigerian man armed with a knife commandeered the cockpit. The Cobra operators quickly subdued the hijacker. Although a criminal rather than political hijacking, this remains the only known case of a CT unit resolving a hijacking whilst in the air, for which Russia's President Putin awarded them medals.

EKO Cobra combat swimmer preparing to board a ship during an MCT exercise; for this mission he wears a lighter ProtTec climbing helmet instead of ballistic headgear. The slung APC9 sub-machine gun, from the Swiss manufacturer, Brügger & Thomet, features ambidextrous controls, a specially designed stock for use with a visored helmet, quad rails to attach lights and lasers, and is even engraved with the unit's logo. (Photo courtesy BM.I/Polizei)

In 2002, after an evaluation of CT capabilities in the wake of the '9/11' attacks, the Austrian government ordered a further reorganization by merging urban and rural SWAT units (13 units of the Mobile Einsatzkommanden or MEK of the Federal Police Directorate, and the eight Special Einsatzgruppen or SEG units of the Landesgendamariekommanden) with GEK Cobra, to achieve uniformity of training and equipment. At this point the renamed EKO Cobra was established.

In 2013 the command was again restructured, with CT investigatory, EOD and surveillance units brought under the one roof alongside EKO Cobra. The organization now has teams totalling more than 700 personnel based across Austria to ensure national coverage. EKO Cobra remain exceptionally busy: in 2015, for example, they conducted some 1,052 tactical operations and over 1,800 close-protection tasks. There is also a separate police tactical unit based in Vienna known as **Wiener Einsatzgruppe Alarmabteilung (WEGA)**, which deals with cases of non-terrorist sieges along with public order, but can operate in support of Cobra.

Belgium

The first Belgian intervention unit was also formed in the aftermath of Munich, in December 1972. It was named Groupe Diane after the Greek goddess of hunting who featured on their insignia, along with the Latin motto 'Ultima Ratio' (roughly, 'The Last Resort'). Once Diane was established the unit conducted a fact-finding mission, visiting numerous CT units in Europe and Israel, leading to expansion in 1973. Groupe Diane was split into two; one element retained the intervention capability, while the other took over the protection of government individuals and facilities from terrorism. With the expansion came a new name, the **Escadron Special d'Intervention (ESI)**, or in Flemish the **Speciaal Interventie Eskadron (SIE)** – under Belgium's constitutional arrangements, and for sheer practicality, a bilingual policy has to be observed.

In 1980, ESI was expanded to some 200 officers. In that year they stormed a school bus that had been seized by criminal hijackers, resolving the situation and saving the hostages without a shot fired. They were also deployed in the hunt for the so-called Nivelles Gang, a murderous group of armed robbers who were terrorizing the country. In the field of counter-terrorism, ESI was particularly active in the mid-1980s against an anti-NATO terrorist group, the Communist Combatant Cells. In 1990, ESI famously captured a PIRA Active Service Unit in their safehouse in Antwerp, recovering small arms and explosives in advance of a visit by Diana, Princess of Wales.

Six years later the unit came up against Algerian GIA terrorists who had escaped from a RAID operation in northern France. They were spotted as they crossed the border and became involved in a gunfight with local police. One terrorist was shot dead before his partner took two hostages in a nearby house. ESI conducted a textbook building assault, capturing him and rescuing both hostages.

ESI was renamed again in 2001 after a restructure of the Federal Police, becoming the **Directorate of Special Units Intervention Unit (DSU)**. In 2007 they became the General Commissariat Special Unit (GCSU), before reverting once more to DSU Intervention Unit in yet another organizational reshuffle in 2014.

The unit has been at the forefront of efforts to combat IS-inspired terrorism in Belgium. In January 2015 the DSU Intervention Unit, supported by members of France's GIGN, killed two terrorists in the Belgian town of Verviers following the *Charlie Hebdo* murders in Paris. The DSU deployed frame charges to blow in the windows of the apartment, but came under immediate and prolonged fire from a number of terrorists armed with AK-47s. After a gunfight lasting several minutes, two terrorists were shot dead and a third surrendered and was taken into custody.

Another operation in March 2016, just before Brussels itself was targeted by a suicide-bomb attack at its international airport, saw Federal Police detectives attempt to question a number of terrorist suspects in the Belgian town of Forest. Instead the officers were engaged by Kalashnikov fire through the front door, and two suspects were then seen fleeing across the roof.

A DSU Quick Reaction Force (QRF) arrived and breached into the apartment, but one operator was wounded by a third, hidden, terrorist, who also engaged a second DSU QRF which was arriving. A siege developed until the terrorist appeared at one of the windows with his rifle raised, and was immediately shot dead by a DSU sniper. A total of four police officers

A sniper from the Belgian DSU Intervention Unit deploys on a rooftop in the town of Forest in support of a March 2016 operation targeting terrorists wanted in connection with the November 2015 atrocities in Paris; one of the gunmen was subsequently shot and killed by a DSU sniper. The weapon is a modified 7.62mm HK G3 battle rifle, with a B&T forward grip with integrated bipod, MSG90 stock and ACOG optic. (Photo Olivier Polet/Corbis via Getty Images)

were wounded in this operation, although none fatally (the Belgian unit have lost three officers killed over the years).

Today's DSU Intervention Unit comprises some 50 operators plus a dozen snipers. It is supported by a number of specialist elements including the Observation Service and the Dog Service. The Observation Service, which began life as the close-protection element of ESI, grew to encompass surveillance, reconnaissance and wilderness tracking. The Observation Service is also home to the unit's negotiators. The Dog Service currently has eight EDDs and two CADs. The ESI were pioneers in the use of dogs in intervention operations, with a canine cell established as early as 1984. Belgian Malinois have also become the primary breed for intervention dogs for the world's special operations forces.

The DSU is supported by a number of satellite units based in major regional centres. These units are known as **Protection, Observation, Support and Arrest (POSA)** teams, and were placed under DSU command in 1995. The POSA can conduct most tactical missions themselves, although hostage-rescue responsibility is retained by the Intervention Unit.

Bosnia-Herzegovina

Counter-terrorism within the combined ex-Yugoslav republic of Bosnia-Herzegovina falls under the auspices of the State Investigation and Protection Agency (SIPA) of the Ministry of Security, a federal unit tasked with combating organized and major crime along with terrorism. Tactical operations are conducted by the SIPA's **Special Support Unit (SSU)** formed in 2005.

The SSU is divided into three distinct sections: Alfa, the Anti-Terrorist Section, which conducts the full range of intervention missions; Beta, the Operations Section, which provides tactical support against non-terrorist armed suspects, along with furnishing dedicated diver, sniper and climbing teams to the SSU; and Gama or Support Section, which provides logistical and technical intelligence support, maintains the unit's vehicle fleet, and houses the SSU's dog section.

Czech operators of the URNA rapid reaction unit and Zasahova Jednotka police SWAT team conduct an assault against a tram during exercises in 2016. The assault ladders are being emplaced under the watchful cover of several officers with MP5s. (Photo Matej Divizna/Getty Images)

Czech Republic

The Rapid Reaction Unit or **Útvar rychlého nasazení (URNA)** is the Czech intervention force. Based in Prague but with a national remit, URNA deals with criminal hostage-takings along with the CT mission. URNA is supported in these roles by the **Zasahova Jednotka (ZJ)**, a regional police SWAT unit. URNA also protects Czech embassies abroad in Iraq, Pakistan and Afghanistan, and carries out close protection for high-risk Czech diplomats.

URNA evolved from a Communist-era Spetsnaz unit and previously used former Warsaw Pact weapons and equipment, but after the fall of the Communist regime in 1989 the unit began to visit other European CT units and adopt best-in-class platforms. Their efforts have resulted in their admission to the European Union's counter-terrorist ATLAS network (see below), including chairing that organization's prestigious sniper forum.

Denmark

Founded in 1972, the 100-man **Politiets Aktionsstyrke (AKS),** known as Action Force, is a part of the Danish Security & Intelligence Service, with responsibility for all police tactical and national CT operations. The AKS today falls under the control of the Security Department, which also houses the negotiation and close-protection units that work closely with Action Force. Like most European intervention units, the AKS has been primarily deployed against criminal rather than terrorist suspects, with one notable exception in February 2015: a wanted terrorist who had killed a Danish film-maker was shot and killed by AKS operators as he opened fire on them during an arrest operation.

The overseas CT mission is handled by the Navy's Frømandskorpset and the Army's Jægerkorpset. Both units primarily conduct reconnaissance and raiding, but also the MCT and CT missions respectively; they have been heavily deployed in Afghanistan.

Eire

The Republic of Ireland maintains both the **Emergency Response Unit (ERU)** of the Garda Siochána national police, and the Irish Army's **Ranger Wing**. The Garda formed a Special Task Force in 1977, heavily influenced by ESI and GSG9; by 1984 this had become the Anti-Terrorist Unit, before becoming the ERU in the late 1980s, when they were heavily committed against PIRA terrorists. The unit has killed a number of terrorists during armed heists designed to finance the terrorist organization; they also famously intercepted a huge truck bomb, and were involved in the arrests of dozens of PIRA members when the ERU stormed two terrorist training camps in 1999 and 2004.

The Ranger Wing was first established in 1980 as the Army's CT unit although, like the Italian GIS, it has expanded its mission set dramatically over the intervening years, to cover all manner of special operations.

Finland

The Finnish Police Rapid Response Unit (**Poliisin Valmiusyksikkö**) is better known as Karhu or the 'Bear Group'. Founded in 1972 amid concerns that terrorists might strike at the 1975 Conference on Security and Cooperation in Europe, it began with a scant 15 officers. Today the unit has over 90 full-time personnel and national responsibility for all CT missions, with its own EOD, canine and negotiation teams.

France

France has a number of intervention units, including the BRI-BAC, RAID and GIGN. Although each has a designated responsibility, today they are integrated into the national CT response plan, enabling the French authorities to respond rapidly to a terrorist incident anywhere on French soil, as part of the National Police Intervention Force (FNIP).

Established in 1966 in response to a wave of violent bank robberies, the **Brigade de Recherche et d'Intervention (BRI)**, under the Ministry of the Interior, is primarily concerned with organized crime, including ransom kidnappings. It has its own Brigade Anti-Commando tactical unit (**BRI-BAC**), trained in hostage-rescue techniques. BRI encompasses both the investigation and tactical arrest of suspects, with members working as detectives before carrying out their own arrests. The Paris-based BRI-BAC was formed to provide domestic CT intervention before RAID was established as the national CT unit in 1985. BRI now has some 300 operators including a negotiation unit, two dog teams and six tactical medics. The BRI-BAC are supported by the so-called Burglary Cell that provides covert breaching expertise. In January 2015 a new unit was established to deal with MTFA incidents such as the *Charlie Hebdo* murders; known as the Quick Reaction Force, this is equipped with motorcycles to weave through the heavy Paris traffic.

The BRI-BAC have been involved in a number of high-profile operations, including the rescue of hostages held in the Bataclan Theatre in Paris on 13 November 2015. As part of a co-ordinated series of attacks across the capital, terrorists seized the Bataclan Theatre during a rock concert and began a massacre, firing indiscriminately and lobbing grenades into the audience. Some 60 members of the BRI-BAC were called to the Bataclan; 40 of these officers prepared to enter the building, while the others established a cordon. Ten additional operators from RAID arrived to support the BRI assault. At 22:15, some 35 minutes after the killings began, the first BRI entry team entered the theatre; they faced a scene from hell, with piles of dead and dying civilians all around them.

By 23:15 they had cleared the ground floor and had moved upstairs, conducting a methodical but grisly tactical search for the remaining terrorists; these were finally located in an upper corridor, cowering behind a door and using hostages as human shields. At 23:30 the BRI's negotiator made first contact with the terrorists. They demanded that the BRI officers withdraw or they would begin decapitating the hostages. Almost an hour later permission for an assault was given, and the team stacked up on the door, which had been left unlocked. The team breached the door, 'posting in' a number of flashbangs and then advancing in a single file behind a Ramses wheeled tactical shield. One terrorist opened fire on the assaulters with his AK-47 as they

Two members of the BRI-BAC assault team that entered the Bataclan Theatre in Paris on 13 November 2015, flanking the central section from a Ramses wheeled ballistic shield (see Plate C) that shows some of the total of 27 AK-47 strikes that hit the three panels. Both officers carry a second Glock on their body armour; the 'shield men' in units such as the BRI-BAC and RAID often partner a full-size Glock 17 with a compact Glock 19 or 26. This allows them to discard the first pistol when empty and draw the other to continue firing immediately, rather than trying to reload while simultaneously controlling the shield. (Photo Kenzo Tribouillard/AFP/Getty Images)

approached, striking the shield some 27 times. An operator in the middle of the stack was struck in the left hand by a round, dropping to the floor and rolling away. Between the BRI operators and the terrorists were some 20 panicked hostages, blocking the team's line of fire. Compounding this, the team encountered some unseen steps that toppled the rolling shield, which fell onto several hostages and left the lead operators dangerously exposed.

Within moments, however, the two gunmen were cornered in a hallway. The BRI team leader explained: 'It was like a dead end for them. The first one blew himself [up] with an explosive jacket. The second one tried to do the same, but was shot by the two first BRI officers.' Further hostages, barricaded in a second room, at first refused to open the door for fear of a terrorist ruse, but eventually these too were freed. The final count showed that 130 people had been murdered at the Bataclan, plus more than 350 wounded.

BRI were also involved in the response to the June 2016 murder by an IS-inspired terrorist of a counter-terrorism officer and his wife, a civilian police employee, at their home. Before the killer could harm the couple's child BRI operators stormed the house and shot him dead. The following month the unit also responded to the grisly murder of a priest during a church service in northern France. After cutting the priest's throat the two terrorists attempted to escape by using nuns as human shields, but the responding BRI operators killed both of them with precision head shots.

Recherche Assistance Intervention Dissuasion (RAID – the designation probably chosen to fit the acronym) is the French National Police's primary hostage-rescue unit. They are known colloquially as the Black Panthers due to their attire (and that feline also now features on the unit's insignia). Formed in 1985, RAID has both the national CT mission within the borders of France (with GIGN – see below – being responsible for overseas missions), and specific responsibility for Paris. For many years RAID worked alongside the regional Groupes d'Intervention de la Police Nationale (GIPN) tactical units which had been formed rapidly in the wake of Munich. The GIPNs were tasked with hostage-rescue and associated CT missions across France, while first the BRI and later RAID took responsibility for Paris. GIPNs served as a regional RAID equivalent until April 2015, when they became RAID Antenna units.

RAID currently has some 400 officers assigned to the unit, more than half of these being based in Paris (including, at the time of writing, two female snipers). The Paris unit is split into three component sections. One is responsible for direct-action interventions, organized into three 25-man teams and including the unit's snipers (known as Omega). The second section is the research and development cell, which also provides technical intelligence support, while the third section comprises the specialist negotiators.

In February 1987, RAID captured four leaders of the Action Directe revolutionary group, and went on to target and capture many key figures within the Basque ETA movement. In 1996 they conducted an early-morning assault on the safehouse of the so-called Gang de Roubaix, an Algerian GIA-linked terrorist group that had conducted a string of violent robberies and murders. RAID carried out an explosive breach on the front door to the safehouse, but one of the entry team was immediately shot by a terrorist inside. Three other terrorists opened fire with AK-47s and began throwing grenades down on the RAID operators, wounding one officer. RAID withdrew and exchanged fire with the terrorists from the street, launching CS gas grenades into the house. One of these set fire to the building, which eventually collapsed as the fire took hold. Four dead terrorists were later found in the rubble.

March 2012 saw RAID kill an IS-inspired terrorist who had murdered three French servicemen in the street, and a Jewish rabbi and three children at a Jewish school in Toulouse. After his location was identified RAID conducted a pre-dawn mission on the suspect's apartment. Unfortunately he was waiting for them and opened fire as the entry team stacked up, hitting three officers and wounding two; the third was saved by his body armour. After a day of negotiation, RAID attempted a second breach, this time using frame charges to blow in a number of windows. They were again met by gunfire, wounding another two officers. Under return fire, the terrorist retreated to the balcony, and as he climbed over it he was shot and killed; examination of the body revealed concealed body armour.

In the wake of the *Charlie Hebdo* massacre of 12 victims in that magazine's Paris offices on 7 January 2015, another terrorist seized the Hyper Cacher kosher supermarket in the suburb of Porte de Vincennes after earlier murdering a policewoman. He murdered four hostages in the initial stages of the incident before the supermarket was surrounded by a combined force of RAID and BRI-BAC, supported by Intervention Brigade public order officers. The supermarket terrorist was in contact with the Kouachi brothers, who were responsible for the *Charlie Hebdo* murders and who were by that time surrounded by GIGN at a print works in Dammartin-en-Goële. Action against either would force an operation against the other. After the Kouachi brothers charged the GIGN lines at Dammartin-en-Goële, RAID and BRI were forced to conduct an assault at the Hyper Cacher.

Deploying flashbangs as a diversion, the assault teams raced towards their entry points. RAID breachers detonated a frame charge against a fire door leading into the rear of the supermarket, but this had been heavily barricaded, impeding entry. The assault at the main entrance became the primary breach, as RAID and BRI officers struggled to raise the metal shutter that had concealed events within. As the shutter was finally raised a flashbang was thrown; a RAID operator carrying a ballistic shield and his Glock was first in, ducking under the shutter. He was alone in the supermarket for some 30 seconds, exchanging fire with the terrorist. He described what he saw in an interview:

'Immediately, I saw the body of a hostage on the ground. Then, about 10 metres in front of me on the other side of the boxes, the suspect emerges with weapons in hand. Everything goes very fast. I go into the store, I saw the hostages on my left. He shoots, his first [rounds] are received against my shield. I continue to progress by returning fire, then I shifted to the right,

E **GIGN AIRCRAFT INTERVENTION; MARIGNANE AIRPORT, MARSEILLE, 26 DECEMBER 1994**

This gives an impression of the external situation around the Airbus A300B registration F-GBEC (Air France Flight 8969) in the closing stage of the operation. (We only show a few representative examples of the cordon personnel gathering around the aircraft by this point.)

(Left to right)

Team 3 have entered the rear right-hand passenger door from airstairs, as have Team 2 on the far side.

Moving forwards, Teams 3 and 2 have opened the middle right-side and forward left-side passenger doors, and have deployed the inflatable escape chutes; they are about to start sending passengers down these.

The final firefight by the depleted Team 1 to clear the cockpit is still in progress, although GIGN snipers (firing from roughly our point of view) have killed the third terrorist inside. A fourth GIGN assault team have raced up the forward airstairs to support Team 1; an operator is about to be sent tumbling back down by a shot from the final terrorist which struck his revolver. **(Diagram)** Deployment of the assault teams, and direction of sniper fire.

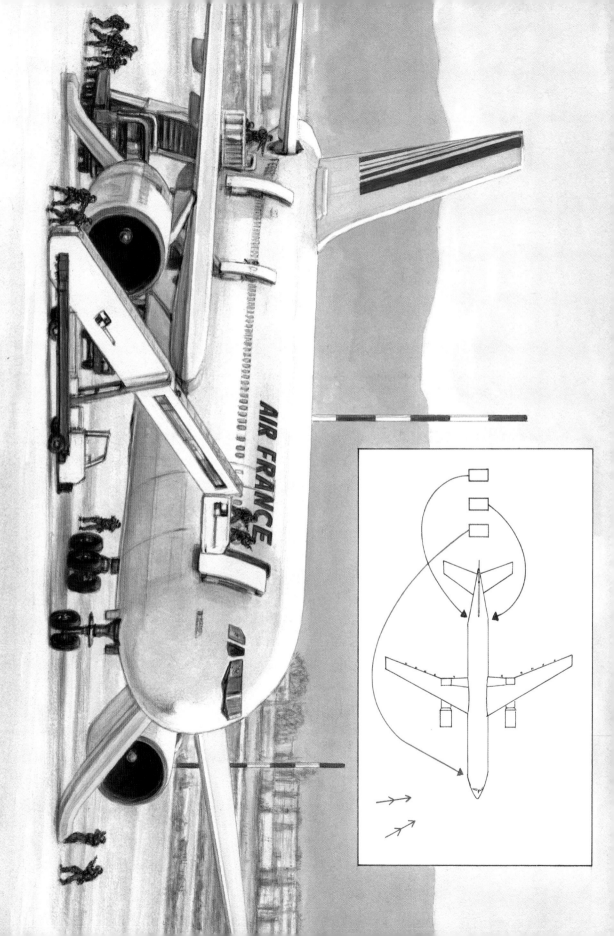

opposite the hostages so that they are not targeted. He then advances towards me, continuing to shoot and I take a round – stopped by the bulletproof vest, but she still hurt... The shooting intensified then as my colleagues stationed behind opened fire in turn.'[4] The terrorist charged the police firing his AK, just as a flashbang detonated inside the doorway. He was gunned down by the RAID and BRI officers, receiving some 40 wounds.

Following the November 2015 wave of terrorist bombings and shootings in Paris, RAID also conducted an operation in the Saint-Denis area, deploying 70 officers. They stormed a terrorist stronghold in an apartment block believed to hold the leader of the terrorist cell (see Plate C). RAID launched their assault with an explosive breach against the target apartment. The commander on the spot explained in an interview with *Le Parisien* newspaper:

'We decided to use explosives to blow off the reinforced door and make the most of the shock effect. It didn't work. The door held and we lost our element of surprise. As a result we had to adapt. We started slowly advancing behind a shield. We came under heavy fire. They fired in bursts or one shot at a time, taking turns so that the gunfire never stopped. They also threw grenades.'[5] The assaulters withdrew; snipers deployed on the perimeter began firing into the apartment, and shot at least one terrorist. Diesel, a combat assault dog fitted with a camera, led a later reconnaissance but was shot and killed. Milkor launchers were then used to fire 40mm grenades in an effort to suppress the terrorists and allow a second breach. The RAID commander continued: 'Carefully we advanced into the apartment. We sent a drone to look through the windows and the skylights, but it did not tell us much.' A UGV with a camera was deployed, but its progress was blocked by rubble. Finally, pole-mounted cameras were pushed up through holes in the floor caused by the grenades and by a suicide vest that had been detonated by one of the terrorists.

'We saw that a body had fallen through the floor. The corpse was damaged as it had been hit by grenades and had been crushed by a beam. It was not identifiable.' The cameras could see no survivors, so RAID cleared the apartment using flashbangs, finally bringing the operation to a close. Some 1,576 rounds were fired by RAID during the battle. Five terrorists were eventually captured, and three died: two from the detonation of a suicide vest, and one asphyxiated under the rubble. Along with the death of their combat assault dog, five members of RAID were wounded; some reports suggest that some may have been struck by police rounds in the confusion.

Unlike RAID, which is part of the National Police, the **Groupe d'Intervention de la Gendarmerie Nationale (GIGN)** is part of the National Gendarmerie, a militarized service subordinate to the Ministry of Defence. Formed in 1974 as the Regional Intervention Commando, it was soon renamed GIGN, and split into two regional commands to provide CT coverage for all of France; two years later it reverted to a unified national command. For much of its early existence GIGN comprised four intervention units of around 20 operators each, supported by a central command group with the unit's dog teams, snipers, and technical surveillance. In 1991 a negotiation cell was added, with two-man teams attached to each intervention group. GIGN are an exceptionally busy unit; they conduct more than 200 operations in an average year, and have rescued more than 600 hostages in total. To cope with increasing demand for their services GIGN have expanded dramatically, including the addition of four GIGN Antenna units drawn from regional tactical units known as Pelotons d'Intervention Interrégional de Gendarmerie or PI2G.

Today GIGN includes the tactical teams now known as Intervention Force (FI), the close protection specialists of the Security Protection Force (FSP), and surveillance teams of the Observation & Research Force (FOR). The FI consists of 100 operators divided into four assault teams. The 80-strong FSP provides physical security for embassies and French diplomats in countries such as Iraq and Afghanistan, and can provide a hostage-rescue capability if required. The 30 men and women of the FOR provide reconnaissance and surveillance capabilities. Most of them are also highly qualified snipers (in fact all GIGN operators complete a basic sniping course, though only the best advance to the full sniper school), mountaineers or combat divers. Reflecting their motto, 'Between the shadow and the light', FOR are also trained in operating undercover. The final operational element of GIGN is the 25-strong Operational Support Force (FAO), which includes specialist breachers, EOD, dog teams, and the Special Means cell which provides technical intelligence-gathering. The FAO also houses a CBRN capability. The Groupe Interarmées d'Hélicoptères, a joint-service military unit flying Puma helicopters, provides aerial support.

GIGN have been involved in numerous famous intervention missions. One of their first was a hostage rescue along the Somali border with Djibouti in 1976, when five terrorists had seized a school bus carrying 30 French children. A resident Foreign Legion subunit from 13e DBLE stopped the bus at the border as it attempted to enter Somalia, and GIGN were dispatched. A plan was developed that would see the children provided with sandwiches dosed with sedatives. Once the drugs took effect, eight GIGN snipers would simultaneously engage all five terrorists with head shots while an assault team from 2nd Co/2eREP (on rotation in Djibouti) stormed the bus and rescued the hostages. Complicating the operation was the fact that nearby Somali border guards were openly sympathetic to the terrorists, and might intervene; the Legion were tasked with ensuring that didn't happen. The operation began with the snipers successfully killing all five hostage-takers. Légionnaires opened fire on the Somali border guards, but as the assault team raced towards the bus a lone Somali managed to fire into it, tragically murdering a five-year-old before he was shot and killed by GIGN. Another child was mortally wounded before the others were rescued.

In 1981, a mentally ill man attempted to set fire to an Aer Lingus flight at Le Touquet. After negotiations stalled, six GIGN officers stormed the aircraft using two assault ladders and captured the hijacker. Two years later, GIGN assaulted a hijacked Iran Air flight at Orly, capturing six terrorists. The following year they resolved another hijacking of an aircraft at Marseille. In 1988, GIGN captured the leader of the Basque ETA terrorist movement, when just two warning shots fired from an MP5 convinced the target of the futility of resistance. Later that year they were instrumental in Operation 'Victor', the rescue of French police officers held hostage by Kanak separatists on the island of New Caledonia in the Pacific; this ended in the deaths of some 19 hostage-takers.

GIGN operators posed beside their Renault Sherpa assault truck fitted with the Patriot 3 HARAS rig. They carry 5.56mm HK416 assault rifles and (right) a 12-gauge Remington breaching shotgun. The central officer's shield is fitted with lights and a camera.
GIGN have recently adopted a new assault rifle following lessons learned after the Paris attacks. To counter terrorists clad in body armour, during 2015 the unit tested a number of 7.62x51mm designs, but due to their size and weight these were judged unsuitable for CQB. Instead GIGN trialled several platforms chambering the Soviet 7.62x39mm round, and eventually selected the Czech CZ806 Bren 2 – with a 9-inch battle, Picatinny rails, and a side-folding SCAR-type stock to gradually replace their HK416s. (Photo Thomas Samson/AFP/Getty Images)

GIGN's most celebrated operation to date was the retaking of the hijacked Air France Flight 8969 at Marseille's Marignane Airport in December 1994. The Airbus A300B, carrying 227 passengers, was hijacked by four terrorists on a Christmas Eve flight from Algiers to Paris. Two hostages were immediately murdered, but negotiators secured the release of 63 others. As complicated politics were played out between the French and Algerian governments, the terrorists demanded to be flown to Paris, and executed another hostage to force the Algerian authorities to allow their departure. During an intermediate landing at Marseille-Marignane to refuel, GIGN operators disguised as maintenance workers entered the aircraft, ascertaining that the doors were not wired with explosives. After the frustrated terrorists opened fire on the control tower, and fearing for the lives of the hostages, on 26 December the GIGN commander on the spot was authorized to launch an intervention, involving three teams assaulting doors by means of mobile 'airstairs' driven up from the blind spot immediately behind the Airbus (see Plate E for the assault teams' deployments).

After encountering a problem with the forward passenger door on the right side, one operator was forced to use his own body weight to operate the locking mechanism. The primary team then entered the aircraft through the forward right-side door behind the cockpit, and what the former GIGN commander called 'a wall of fire' struck the operators: 'six of my men fell wounded before my eyes as soon as we entered'.

Armed with Manurhin MR73 revolvers, Team 1 headed right for the cockpit, and immediately the leading man was faced with an open door and terrorists interspersed with the flight crew. He managed to hit two out of three before a hidden fourth terrorist opened fire on him with an AK-47. He was hit seven times, including once in the face, shattering his helmet's visor. A flashbang thrown by the cordon team missed the cockpit, detonating on the tarmac. The terrorists responded with their own grenades; the wounded lead assaulter was struck by many fragments, which destroyed his right hand. He would lie helpless, with bullets flying over him, for another 12 painful minutes until the operation was concluded.

The firefight continued outside the cockpit: 'I occasionally glimpsed part of the face of one of the shooters through a gap in the door, or a hand that threw a grenade,' recalled the commander.[6] Eventually the Air France co-pilot managed to escape by dropping through the right-side cockpit window, though breaking both legs when he hit the tarmac far below; this allowed external GIGN snipers to fire into the cockpit, killing another terrorist. Meanwhile, Teams 2 and 3 had entered from airstairs pushed against the two rear passenger doors. Moving forwards, they released two other doors from the inside, deployed the inflatable escape chutes, and began shepherding the passengers down them. When a final assault team raced up the front right-hand steps to support their colleagues outside the cockpit, the last terrorist fired on them, striking one officer's revolver and sending him tumbling back down before he himself was finally shot.

The operation had lasted 22 minutes. Eleven GIGN officers were wounded, one gravely, although he later rejoined the unit as a firearms instructor; 13 passengers and crew were injured, but all hostages were safely released, in what became a benchmark for counter-hijacking operations.

GIGN were also instrumental in neutralizing the perpetrators of the *Charlie Hebdo* killings in January 2015. After the two terrorist brothers were located at a print works in Dammartin-en-Goële north of Paris, GIGN surrounded the building. Only one employee remained hidden in the building unbeknownst to the terrorists after they had released the owner. The former commander of GIGN during the assault on Air France Flight 8969, Denis Favier, was now in charge of the Gendarmerie and was unequivocal in his briefing to GIGN: 'the aim is to neutralize them without getting our people killed. If we can't neutralize them, then we destroy them. If we can take them alive, so much the better.' Shortly after 17:00, GIGN snipers registered movement inside the building as the assault teams awaited the final order to storm it. Instead, the brothers exited the front door of the print works, guns blazing. GIGN snipers began engaging them as the cordon team launched flashbangs at the suicidal pair of jihadists; 90 seconds later the brothers lay dead. In case any other terrorists remained, GIGN launched an immediate assault using their Sherpa intervention vehicles to insert assaulters into the second floor. They blew in the window with a frame charge and rescued the sole hostage before methodically clearing the building. A live grenade was discovered concealed under the body of one terrorist in a final attempt to kill more police.

A 2015 image of a GSG9 officer on a rappel rope, covering a window with his Glock 17 with mounted light; he also carries a 5.56mm HK416 assault rifle with EOTech optic. Note the Ops Core helmet, and the latest Crye uniform with matching olive drab Lindnerhof Taktik plate carrier. Prior to 2015 the unit favoured black Crye or Arc'teryx uniforms with olive drab or MultiCam camouflage plate carriers. (Photo courtesy Bundespolizei/GSG9)

Germany

On 26 September 1972, barely weeks after the disaster at Munich, a national intervention unit was established by the German Minister of the Interior. It was important domestically that the unit be raised from the police rather than the military, to avoid any historical echoes of wartime elite units, and thus the new unit was placed within the Bundesgrenzschutz or Federal Border Guard Service. It was named **Grenzschutzgruppe 9 (GSG9)**.

Its first leader, Col (now Gen) Ulrich 'Ricky' Wegener, worked with both the British SAS and the Israeli Sayaret Matkal in developing the unit, based at St Augustin near Bonn. He organized GSG9 into three combat sub-units: GSG9/1, which maintains the hostage rescue capability and the unit's sniper programme; GSG9/2, which specializes in MCT including combat diving, submersibles and small boats; and GSG9/3, which focuses on aerial operations, including HAHO and HALO parachuting. Each of these Combat Units was further split into five-man assault teams known as Sonder Einsatztrupp (SETs).

GSG9's first intervention mission was Operation Feuerzauber ('Fire Magic'), to rescue the passengers and crew of Lufthansa Flight LH181, a Boeing 737 hijacked by four PFLP terrorists en-route to Frankfurt from Spain on 13 October 1977. The operation has received much analysis (including the Osprey title RAID 19, *Storming Flight 181: GSG 9 and the Mogadishu Hijack* by Chris McNab), so we will limit ourselves here to a brief overview. After criss-crossing the Middle East, the hijacked flight ended up landing at Mogadishu, Somalia. After the pilot was murdered, GSG9 was given the authority to conduct an intervention on 18 October. Two members of the British SAS accompanied the team: Maj Alastair Morrison, a veteran of the legendary 'battle of Mirbat' in Oman, and Sgt Barry Davies. Wegener clarified a few details in a 2012 interview:

'The German government asked two members of the British SAS to provide us with flashbang grenades. They gave us the grenades in Dubai, but we discovered that we could not use them in the plane because they contained phosphorus, which could burn the passengers and also start a fire. We took the flashbangs with us but we decided not to use them. A lot of stories circulate about this episode but this is the pure truth.' Along with a number of MP5s, the primary assaulters were equipped with pistols: 'We also had [the] H&K P9S and .357 Magnum Smith & Wesson. Only some of the men were wearing flak jackets, because we had not enough. Personally I was not wearing any flak jacket because I thought it was more important for my men.'[7] Snipers with night vision equipment had identified the location of at least two of the terrorists before six GSG9 teams began their careful, stealthy approach. Once all were in position, the Somalis were told to light a bonfire further up the tarmac as a distraction. While the terrorists' attention was drawn to the fire, the assault ladders were placed and Wegener gave the order. A former GSG9 officer explained in a 2012 interview:

'We put the ladders on. We could only communicate by hand [signals], we could not even whisper. We also had radio problems, that is, we were not fully informed about the negotiations with the terrorists. We also had to be prepared for explosives on the doors [in which case] we would die immediately we opened them. In that case, the reserve groups were already ready to storm [the aircraft].'[8] At the codeword 'Fire Magic', the assaulters, dressed in jeans and tee-shirts with Bristol body armour but without helmets, forced the doors open and swept into the airliner, shouting 'Heads down!' in German and English.

Two terrorists were immediately shot; one was killed in the cockpit while the other, standing in the gangway, was hit by five rounds but survived. A third terrorist was shot as he awoke from sleep in the first class cabin, but not before he threw two grenades. Luckily they detonated under the seats and caused only slight wounds to two hostages. The last terrorist attempted to hide in a toilet, but Wegener himself opened fire through the door, killing her. The code word 'Spring Time' was transmitted, indicating 'aircraft secured'. One GSG9 officer was wounded by a bullet which grazed his neck, and

The olive drab Crye uniform and Lindner Taktik plate carrier and the MultiCam Ops Core helmet currently worn by GSG9 show up clearer in this torchlit image. Front and rear men carry Glock 17s with lights mounted, the middle officer the HK416, which is replacing the G36C in service with the unit. (Photo courtesy Bundespolizei/GSG9)

three passengers were slightly wounded, during an operation lasting seven minutes. Wegener later put the success of the operation into context: 'It was the result of successful training. We had practised this for many years.'

GSG9 were heavily involved in the fight against Red Army Faction (RAF), whose logo ironically featured the MP5, a weapon that would become synonymous with CT units. In 1982, GSG9 captured two key members of the group as they arrived at a weapons cache. Ten years later, GSG9 were also involved in an operation to capture two RAF leaders at a railway station in Bad Kleinen. When GSG9 challenged the terrorists, one opened fire, hitting and killing a GSG9 officer and wounding another. It was later alleged that the terrorist was subsequently executed by GSG9, but an inquest ruled that he had in fact committed suicide with his own weapon. Any lingering stain on the unit was removed several weeks later, when GSG9 deployed in response to a hijacked Dutch KLM airliner at Düsseldorf. The hostage-taker, an Egyptian, was captured alive without a shot fired.

Typical uniform and equipment of officers from a German police regional SWAT team or Sonder Einsatzkommando (SEK), *c.* 1998. They wear the Ulbrichts AM-95 visored helmet, and Adidas GSG9 boots. The weapons are an MP5A3 sub-machine gun with a Streamlight forearm and what looks like an elderly Armson OEG red-dot optic, and a Swiss 9mm SIG P226 pistol. (Photo Spiegl/ullstein bild via Getty Images)

In the aftermath of the '9/11' attacks in 2001, GSG9 were heavily deployed in the hunt for the support cell for the hijackers. Two GSG9 officers assigned to close protection duties in Iraq were killed in 2004 after their convoy was ambushed outside Fallujah; their armoured SUV was struck by an RPG, killing both officers.

By the time of GSG9's 40th anniversary the unit had conducted more than 1,700 operations. GSG9's commanding officer at the time noted: 'This may be surprising; we have only used firearms seven times since our founding 40 years ago. A precisely planned and carried-out operation is usually sufficient to leave the suspect without options. Unfortunately, this was not always the case. Remember that three of our comrades lost their lives in operations, two of them in Iraq, protecting German embassy members.'

Another German police intervention unit was formed in 2015, known as the **Beweissicherungs und Festnahmeeinheit Plus (BFE+)**. This new 50-member unit based in Berlin provides CT tactical support to the police alongside the SEKs and MEKs (regionally based SWAT units), as well as supporting GSG9. The German Army established its own special operations unit after German citizens became trapped in war-torn Rwanda in 1994; this crisis reaction unit was designated **Kommando Spezialkräfte (KSK)**. Along with this capability, KSK was given the overseas CT mandate. KSK expanded into a full-spectrum special operations unit, deploying to Afghanistan and later in the fight against Islamic State in Iraq.

Greece

The Greek **Eidikes Katastaltikes Antitromokratikes Monades (EKAM)** was founded in 1984 by the merger of two earlier police CT units. Under the auspices of the National Police, EKAM has had a number of significant operations, including arresting key members of the 17 November terrorist group, and the successful assault of a hijacked Turkish airliner in 2003. As the after-action review briskly stated: 'At 03:30 hours, the Greek Police Special

A dynamic demonstration of a bus assault by the Greek EKAM unit: a diversionary charge is detonating ahead of the bus, while the assaulters race in aboard their modified SUVs. (Photo courtesy Hellenic Police)

Forces made an assault on the aircraft and found the hijacker at the cockpit. We used the [Taser] M26. The hijacker fell immediately to the floor and was successfully arrested.'

Hungary

The Hungarian Counter-Terrorism Centre (**TEK**) of the Interior Ministry was founded in 2010 to bring together disparate CT resources, and is today based in Budapest. The national CT intervention role is managed by their Operations Directorate, with six teams based in the capital and seven based regionally. The TEK is also home to the Intelligence Directorate, which investigates terrorist suspects, and the Personal Protection Directorate, tasked with close protection of government facilities and officials.

Italy

Italy maintains two CT intervention units: the **Gruppo di Intervento Speciale** (**GIS**) of the Carabinieri, which is a militarized gendarmerie; and the **Nucleo Operativo Centrale di Sicurezza** (**NOCS**) of the National Police.

The GIS was founded in 1978, and tasked with overseas interventions along with certain categories of domestic operations such as airliner hijackings. Since 2004 GIS missions have been dramatically expanded to include full-spectrum special operations while maintaining their CT capability. Divided into three intervention units and one sniper cell, GIS strength currently stands at around 150 operators, who are recruited exclusively from the Carabinieri's parachute battalion. In 1985 GIS operators were on standby alongside SEAL Team 6 to conduct a joint assault on the hijacked cruise ship *Achille Lauro*, and also operated extensively against the Red Brigades. They are perhaps best known for the successful rescue of a number of prison guards held hostage in 1980, but have also operated in the Balkans, Iraq and Afghanistan.

In this image dating from the late 1980s, NOCS operators display a range of their then-current weapons and equipment. Visible are both suppressed MP5SD3 and Beretta PM12-S2 sub-machine guns, and 12-gauge SPAS-12 and SPAS-15 shotguns. These shotguns were innovative weapons for their time, offering both pump and magazine-fed semi-automatic modes. (Photo courtesy NOCS)

The NOCS or Central Security Operations Unit of the Italian National Police has the primary responsibility for homeland CT intervention. Formed as Nucleus Anticommando in 1974 to provide a tactical capability for the police Anti-Terrorism Bureau, it was expanded to 50 officers in 1978 and renamed NOCS. The unit are known informally as 'Leatherheads' due to their early helmets. Their well-known Latin motto 'Sicut Nox Silentes' means 'Silent as the night'.

During the 1970s and 1980s the unit conducted dozens of operations against Red Brigade terrorists, of which the most famous was Operation 'Winter Harvest', the successful rescue of kidnapped US Gen James Dozier in 1982. In 1990 their mission set was expanded to include close protection of government personnel and facilities. NOCS are currently organized into five operational units: four tasked with intervention, and a fifth dedicated to close protection. They maintain their own combat diving and dog teams, and members are trained in freefall parachuting. The 140-man unit recently became part of the newly developed Special Operations Division, where it sits alongside the national police EOD and marksman units.

NOCS operator conducting a maritime counter-terrorist exercise aboard a US Navy ship. He wears a full CBRN suit under his assault coveralls. (Photo Photographer's Mate 3rd Class John Roark/courtesy US Navy)

Lithuania

The Lithuanian Police Anti-terrorist Operations Unit or **Aras** came into being in 1991, and provides tactical support against organized crime, close protection and public order. Aras is divided into three geographically dispersed teams: the Special Intervention Unit, 1st Intervention Division and 2nd Intervention Division. The Lithuanian military's Special Purpose Service, founded in 1997, conducts the overseas CT mission.

The Netherlands

The **Bijzondere Bijstands Eeinheid (BBE)** of the Royal Netherlands Marine Corps was founded in 1973 in the wake of Munich. The BBE was redesignated the Unit Interventie Mariniers (UIM) in 2006, but is still widely known by its former title.

After they rescued a number of hostages being held by rioting prisoners in 1974, in June 1977 the unit performed their first CT intervention, a mission that was destined to become a classic that would be studied for years to come. A month earlier nine South Moluccan terrorists seized a train carrying 54 hostages at De Punt in Drenthe province, north-east Netherlands. Simultaneously, four other terrorists seized a nearby primary school, taking 110 hostages. At the school, police managed to place laxatives in the food delivered for the children, who were consequently released by their captors after suffering the ill effects. Just four teachers remained as hostages.

Negotiations dragged on for an incredible three weeks, but interventions at both sites were finally authorized after the terrorists murdered the train driver. (The train operation on 11 June is detailed in Plate F.) Soon afterwards an assault commenced on the school, with an armoured car ramming walls to disorientate the terrorists. An explosive breach enabled the BBE entry team to capture all four terrorists without a firefight. The terrorists had apparently heard of the assault on the train, and were keen to avoid their compatriots' fate.

A year later, 69 hostages were taken in a three-storey government building in Assen on 13 March 1978. After a hostage was murdered the BBE made a covert breach into the basement of the building while negotiations were continuing. The following day, after the terrorists announced the imminent murder of further hostages, the BBE struck, fighting their way up from the basement while also storming the building from outside. All three hostage-takers were captured, but one hostage later died of wounds.

In 2004 the BBE deployed in support of a police Arrestatieteam (one of the municipal and regional tactical units of the Dutch police) after an attempt to arrest a number of terrorism suspects from the Dutch domestic jihadist group, Hofstadgroep, had gone disastrously wrong. A reinforced door at the group's safehouse had stalled the Arrestatieteam long enough for a terrorist to lob a grenade amongst them, wounding five officers. The house was surrounded by BBE and snipers from the **Brigade Speciale Beveiligingsopdrachten (BSB)**, the tactical unit of the Royal Netherlands Marechaussee (the Dutch gendarmerie). When CS gas was deployed the two terrorists were forced to emerge onto a balcony. When one appeared to be reaching for a weapon a sniper shot and wounded him, before the BBE captured both men.

Today, renamed as UIM, the Marine unit forms part of the joint command termed Dienst Speciale Interventies (DSI), which manages all CT activities. Along with the UIM, the DSI coordinates the police Arrestatieteams and the Marechaussee's BSB. The DSI also has a separate element known as the Expertise & Operational Support Unit; this provides technical support and intelligence, a dedicated sniper unit, and a canine team with seven dogs. The DSI can deploy a combined unit of Arrestatieteam officers and UIM Marines known as the Unit Interventie (UI). The UI responds to most terrorist incidents, and will be used to effect the capture of armed terrorist suspects. However, under the DSI the 130-man UIM has sole responsibility for particularly complex or expansive CT operations, including maritime missions, large-scale hostage takings, and hijacked aircraft and trains.

F **DUTCH BBE TRAIN INTERVENTION; DE PUNT, 11 JUNE 1977**

Overview

Combat divers had swum along the canal that paralleled the left side of the tracks; they had covertly placed surveillance equipment, and an explosive charge at the head of the train (right). By dawn on 11 June, snipers were monitoring the locations of the nine terrorists and of their hostages. The latter had been segregated by gender into two compartments: the first-class compartment behind the locomotive, and the front part of the second coach, ahead of the dining compartment. The terrorists were confirmed as being ahead of the first-class compartment, in the rear of the second coach, and with individual sentries between and behind these **(see diagram)**. Ready to 'shoot the assault parties in', a total of three machine-gunners and 21 snipers were in position under cover, spread along the right of the front half of the train and ahead of the locomotive.

When the order was given to commence, six waiting F-104 fighter jets of the Royal Netherlands Air Force engaged afterburners and buzzed the train at treetop level, making a deafening and disorientating noise and even shattering windows. At the same time the charge ahead of the locomotive was triggered, as another diversion. Then the BBE machine-gunners and snipers opened fire from the right and ahead; most of the terrorists were killed or badly wounded by this fusillade, only two escaping injury. Sadly, one hostage was also killed by sniper fire.

Inset & diagram

Marine BBE teams armed with Uzis and grenades then assaulted from the left side blowing their way in with charges jammed against the doors with timber beams. One group's charge failed to detonate, forcing them to smash their way in through windows. The groups then turned left and right and worked their way through the compartments. The team that entered the dining car encountered one female terrorist, who was immediately engaged and killed. The team heading for the hostages came across two dead and two badly wounded terrorists; both of the latter quickly surrendered. As the BBE team reached the hostages one operator was shot and wounded by a surviving terrorist hiding among them. Tragically, a hostage then fled for the exit in panic, and was killed in the crossfire. The terrorist was subdued with a concussion grenade, and captured.

Within three minutes, the BBE had secured the hostages and had either killed or captured all nine terrorists. Apart from the two hostages who lost their lives, six others and two Marines were wounded.

= terrorist

= hostages

= BBE assaulters

= MG & sniper fire

Polish SPAP operators conduct a joint exercise with German SEK teams in 2013. The SPAP officers wear black coveralls and carry 9mm H&K UMP SMGs, while their German colleagues wear grey and carry MP5s. (Photo Joern Haufe/Getty Images)

Norway

The **Beredskapstroppen (Emergency Response Unit), or Delta** are the Norwegian police intervention unit. They can be supported by the Army's Forsvarets Spesialkommando (FSK), who also have overseas CT responsibilities. The Navy's Marinejegerkommandoen (MJK) are tasked with MCT, primarily around the security of oil rigs. Delta has mainly operated against criminal hostage-takers and organized crime rather than terrorists. One of its snipers ended a siege in 1994 with a precision shot killing a hostage-taker as Delta assaulters stormed the Sandefjord Airport to capture a second hostage-taker and free their captives, who included a police negotiator. They were also the unit that responded (though sadly, after the event) to the mass shooting and bomb attacks by the neo-Nazi domestic terrorist Anders Behring Breivik, who murdered 77 people in Oslo and on Utoya Island on 22 July 2011.

Poland

Poland maintains a national response unit within the National Policja called the **Biuro Operacji Antyterrorystycznych (BOA)** or Anti-Terrorist Bureau, who have primary CT responsibility within Poland's borders. The unit grew from the Communist-era Faculty of Security established in the mid-1970s, and initially consisted of just 47 officers divided into five assault sections. With a counter-hijacking responsibility added to their mandate, the unit expanded dramatically in 1982 and again in 1990, being renamed the BOA in 2003 and joining the international ATLAS network (see below) the following year.

In 1996 the unit lost their first operator in a terrorist bombing, and two further officers were killed in 2003, when the unit conducted an assault against two heavily armed criminals equipped with IEDs. The after-action review of the incident led to the unit receiving heavy body armour, PKM medium machine guns for suppressive fires, and grenade launchers.

Today the 250-man unit is divided into two Battle Divisions of four assault teams with an attached marksman section. The Operational Support

Division includes negotiators and a reconnaissance and surveillance cell, while Technical Support provides technical intelligence. The unit also has its own tactical medics, EOD, and CBRN specialist advisors. The BOA are supported by the **Samodzielny Pododdział Antyterrorystyczny Policji (SPAP)**, regional police intervention teams in a similar vein to the GIGN Antenna units in France.

The Polish Army has the famous **Grupa Reagowania Operacyjno Manewrowego (GROM** – which also fittingly means 'thunderbolt' in Polish), a full-spectrum SOF unit that has close ties to the British SAS and American Delta Force. Founded in 1990, GROM has conducted many special operations in Kosovo, Iraq and Afghanistan, while maintaining a strong CT capability and responsibility for the overseas CT missions. Organized into three SAS-like squadrons, GROM assault teams comprise six operators trained in 'black tactics' (CT operations), 'green tactics' (special operations), and 'blue tactics' (maritime operations). Although GROM have the international mission, they may also be called upon to support the BOA and SPAP, as for instance during the precautionary planning for the Euro 2012 soccer tournaments.

Portugal

The **Grupo de Operações Especiais (GOE)** or Special Operations Group of the Portuguese Public Security Police was founded in 1982, and their first major operation occurred in 1983, when the Turkish ambassador's residence was seized by Armenian terrorists. As GOE prepared their assault the terrorists accidentally detonated explosives they had placed around the building, killing all of the terrorists and two hostages.

Today the unit is organized into three Grupos Operacionais de Intervenção, assault units of two dozen operators each, supported by the Grupo Operacional Técnico; based on similar principles to GIGN's Force Operational Support, this provides technical surveillance, canine, and EOD support.

Soldiers of the Polish Army's GROM unit conduct an explosive breach using a frame charge, during NATO counter-terrorism exercises in 2014. They wear Crye MultiCam uniforms and Ops Core helmets, and carry 5.56mm HK416 assault rifles with EOTech optics. (Photo Michal Fludra/NurPhoto/Corbis via Getty Images)

Romania

The Romanian **Serviciul Independent de Interventii si Actiuni Speciale (SIIAS)** grew from a tactical unit within the Romanian Police's Organized Crime Brigade. The SIIAS is divided into the Department for Special Interventions and Actions, comprising two 30-man intervention units, and the Department for Pyrotechnics, which handles both explosive breaching and EOD. The SIIAS is supported by a Gendarmerie unit known as the **Brigada Specială de Intervenție a Jandarmeriei (BSIJ)**, which was created in 2003 and developed with the assistance of GIGN.

Russia

(Extensive material on Russian units is available in Osprey's Elite 197 *Russian Security and Paramilitary Forces since 1991*, and Elite 206 *Spetsnaz*, both by Mark Galeotti.)

The primary Russian intervention unit is **Spetsgruppa A**, better known as the **Alfa Unit**, of the Federal Security Service (FSB). Alfa (or Alpha) traces its origins to a unit founded back in 1974 by the KGB to provide the Soviet Union's CT intervention capability. Their motto roughly translates as 'Where Alpha appears, compromise stops.'

Alfa is split into two detachments, which are further divided into platoons of around 30 operators. Along with CT they also conduct covert SOF missions, which saw them deployed to Afghanistan during the Soviet occupation. Alfa are also assigned high-risk close protection tasks, whilst Spetsgruppa B (Vympel) guards sensitive facilities. Alfa has conducted a number of hostage-rescue missions, including a counter-hijacking operation in Georgia in 1983. They have also deployed on nominally police operations that involved foreign hostages. Although originally based on military Spetsnaz methods, the unit has developed Western-style tactics and techniques and could now be considered the equal of many European units.

Much of Alfa's evolution has come at a grim price, since the elimination of terrorists has always been a higher priority than the survival of hostages. For example, at the Budennovsk Hospital in 1995 some 130 hostages were

A team from Russia's Spetsgruppa A stacking up outside a target. All these Alfa operators carry the selective-fire VSS Vintorez carbine, an integrally suppressed weapon that fires a unique 9x39mm round which is available in both subsonic and armour-piercing configurations. Their sidearms are difficult to discern, but seem to include at least one Stechkin APS machine pistol; this has been popular within the unit, although today largely replaced with Glock pistols. The helmet is the fibreglass Sphere Lynx-T design with ballistic visor. (Photo courtesy SpetsnazAlpha)

killed in a bloody operation against Chechen terrorists. Alfa were also present at the infamous Dubrovka Theatre and Beslan school sieges, both of which ended with significant losses amongst the hostages.

Serbia

The Serbian **Specijalna Antiteroristicka Jedinica (SAJ)** is that nation's primary intervention force, under the Ministry of Internal Affairs. Established in 1978, it gained notoriety during the Kosovo conflict, when it was alleged to have been involved in a number of atrocities. A second intervention force known as the Protivteroristička Jedinica (PTJ) existed within the National Police until 2015, when it was merged with the SAJ. The SAJ is today divided into four distinct units, bearing some similarity to EKO Cobra or GSG9: two are dedicated intervention teams, another is composed of snipers, dog handlers, combat divers, and the EOD cell, while the fourth provides close protection.

Slovakia

The Slovakian Ministry of the Interior's intervention unit is called **Útvar Osobitného Určenia (UOU)**, but is better known as the Lynx Commando due to that animal featuring on the unit's insignia. The unit began life as part of the Czech URNA before the separation of Slovakia from Czechoslovakia in 1993, and became the primary Slovakian CT intervention unit in 1996. The overseas CT mission is the responsibility of the Army's 5th Special Forces Regt, who train alongside Lynx. Lynx's most famous mission was the 2007 seizure of smuggled radioactive material that it was feared was intended for a terrorist 'dirty bomb'; Lynx conducted the arrest, and recovered half a kilogram of powdered uranium.

Spain

Formed in 1977, the Spanish **Grupo Especial de Operaciones (GEO)** is the National Police's CT intervention unit. From its inception GOE has had close ties with GSG9, and Col Wegener and a training cell from the German

HM King Felipe VI of Spain visiting the GEO; the police officers wear their distinctive sea-green coveralls and visored helmets. The sniper (right) carries a suppressed 7.62mm HK417, and the assaulters MP5s fitted with B&T stocks, Aimpoint optics, and a variety of lights and lasers. (Photo Pablo Cuadra/WireImage)

unit were instrumental in its initial organization and equipping. No such unit had ever existed in Spain before, so everything, including recruitment of suitable operators, had to be built up from scratch. By 1979 the unit was considered operational.

The GEO is organized into an Operations Section and a logistical and administrative Support Section. The Operations Section is further split into two groups: Operational Action Group (OAG) 40, and OAG 50. Each of these OAGs has three five-man operational teams among a total of 30 personnel per OAG. They specialize in breaching, sniping, combat diving or surveillance. To date, the GEO has captured 41 terrorists and rescued some 424 hostages. It has also been involved in more than 20 missions at sea. Like many of its contemporaries, it also conducts high-risk close protection of diplomats, embassies and consulates around the world. In April 2004, in the wake of the Madrid train bombings that killed 192 civilians, GEO lost an operator killed as the unit pursued the terrorists responsible.

Switzerland

The Swiss maintain a small Federal Police unit that operates against armed criminals and terrorists. Known as **Einsatzgruppe Tigris**, this existed in secrecy for almost a decade. Tigris works in concert with municipal police tactical units, or as the primary intervention force for terrorist incidents on Swiss soil. Switzerland also has the Army Reconnaissance Detachment 10 (ARD10) responsible for overseas CT missions, non-combatant evacuations, special reconnaissance and similar missions. Like the German KSK, it is a relatively new unit, activated in 2003 and also structured upon an SAS model.

The separate cantonal police units are themselves very well trained and equipped, and have been responsible for a number

A sniper of Switzerland's Argus intervention unit from the canton of Aargau, which has proved itself in competition with GSG9. He wears a 'ghillie suit' for the rural environment, and carries a suppressed 7.62mm SIG716 with the Schmidt & Bender PMII optic. Unusually, the sound suppressor is a custom design manufactured by the unit's snipers. (Photo courtesy SE Argus)

G
BRITAIN & FRANCE, since 2015
(1) British 22 SAS Pagoda Team
In contrast to Plate A2 from 1980, this figure is based upon much more recent imagery. Although the SAS have been seen wearing black Crye uniforms in the Special Projects role, they have also been observed wearing this Crye MultiCam uniform (with a UBACS shirt) while on CT exercises within the UK. This trooper appears to be wearing an Ops Core helmet fitted with both an infra-red strobe at the rear and night vision goggles, and a Crye Jumpable Plate Carrier (JPC) for body armour, also in MultiCam. Note his Individual First Aid Kit (IFAK) at the rear, and, hanging behind his left side, a plastic bag of chemlights. His assault rifle is the 5.56mm Colt Canada L119A2, fitted with a Trijicon ACOG magnified optic, a back-up red-dot sight for closer range, and an ATPIAL illuminator. The sidearm, in what appears to be a Safariland ALS holster, is a 9mm Glock 19 with magazine extender.
(2) French GIGN
This Gendarmerie Nationale operator was illustrated as the unit deployed to Dammartin-en-Goële following the *Charlie*

Hebdo massacre in January 2015; the Kouachi brothers were killed there when they made a suicidal charge against GIGN. He wears navy-blue Arc'teryx coveralls and GSG9 boots. As a member of the containment team, he carries both a 40mm Milkor MGL grenade launcher, and a 5.56mm HK416 assault rifle fitted with an Aimpoint optic (mounted unusually forward) and a 3x magnifier.
(3) British CTSFO, Metropolitan Police SCO19
This officer is a sniper from the recently formed Counter Terrorist Specialist Firearms Officer unit within SCO19. On his Arc'teryx coveralls in 'wolf-grey', note the 'Metropolitan Police' sleeve-patches, identifying his number within the team and – by the coloured corner – the team itself (sergeants also display their chevrons on these patches). Over this he wears a C2RMOR plate carrier made by C2R of Hereford, who also manufacture such items for UK Special Forces. SCO19 have now upgraded their sniper rifles to this bolt-action 7.62mm Accuracy International AT308 with a compact 20in barrel. His pistol is the usual Glock 17, in a Safariland drop holster.

of significant operations including the 1984 recapture of a hijacked Air France airliner. Units such as Bern's Enzian and Geneva's GIGG have been in existence since 1972, while the Argus unit from Aargau has sometimes placed ahead of the likes of GSG9 in international competitions.

United Kingdom

Responsibility for interventions within the UK today rests with the police, and in the London area specifically with the Metropolitan Police's SCO19, supported by regional firearms units. In this role they are supported if necessary by UK Special Forces, including the Special Air Service (SAS), Special Boat Service (SBS), and the Special Forces Support Group (SFSG). UK Special Forces maintain the overseas CT mission; historically, however, the SAS have held the primary responsibility for CT interventions within the UK up until relatively recently. (Much of the history of the **SAS** role in CT is documented in the present author's Osprey Elite 211, *The SAS 1983–2014*, so to avoid duplication we will only briefly cover the key points here.)

Originally known as Pagoda Troop after the name of the SAS' fledgling CT programme (Operation 'Pagoda'), the role was assigned to the Regiment's Counter Revolutionary Warfare (CRW) Wing just days after the 1972 Munich disaster. Within weeks, a 20-man unit, drawn largely from the SAS's Bodyguarding Cell, was formed. Training was conducted in a purpose-built, six-room indoor range termed the Close Quarter Battle House at the Pontrilas Army Training Area (known within the SAS as the 'Killing

A recent image of a 22 SAS Special Projects team apparently taken during 2015 exercises in Jordan, with HM King Abdullah himself (centre). Note the black Crye uniforms, Ops Core helmets, and the recently issued Colt Canada L119A2 assault rifles. The facemasks are to protect against the effects of Simunition training ammunition. (Photographer unknown; private collection)

House'). This facility has been rebuilt and renovated numerous times over the years, and now offers full 360° shooting, moveable walls and furniture to create any required scenario, and closed circuit video monitoring to allow immediate critiques. Drills in the Killing House often include live hostages and always employ live ammunition and munitions. VIPs including the Royal Family must undergo hostage training in the facility so that they will know what to expect should they be seized and the SAS is called upon to intervene. (Princess Diana famously had her hair set alight by a spark from a flashbang, leading to a new hairstyle that set the fashion pages aflutter.)

Maritime CT fell to the SBS; their unique waterborne skills made them ideal candidates for the role, and the modest size of the SAS Pagoda Troop prevented their taking responsibility for both land- and sea-based incidents. The Royal Marines established their own unit (Commachio Company) to retake North Sea oil rigs in support of the SBS.

The SAS received their first call-out on 7 January 1975 to a hijacked airliner at Stansted Airport under Operation 'Snowdrop', the codename for SAS support to the police. The team easily overpowered the Iranian hijacker with no shots fired. More seriously, they were also deployed to London early in December that year, when four members of a six-man PIRA Active Service Unit (who had murdered, among others, an unarmed police constable, and the journalist Ross McWhirter in front of his family) were surrounded by the police in a flat in Balcombe Street, Marylebone, where they had taken the two residents hostage. The Metropolitan Police D11 Firearms Unit had deployed, but the SAS were called in under the provisions of the Military Aid to the Civil Authorities legislation to conduct a proposed assault. When news of their arrival featured on the evening news on 12 December, which

Posing with their BMW motorcycles, British CTSFOs of the Metropolitan Police's SCO19 show their latest 'wolf-grey' Arc'teryx uniforms, C2RMOR plate carriers, and 5.56mm SIG516 rifles; compare with Plate G3. SCO19 have also recently adopted the 5.56mm SIG MCX compact carbine with collapsible stock. The helmets carry a team letter and individual number; the number is repeated on the dark blue sleeve patches, which have corners in team colours. After the May 2017 suicide bombing in Manchester, UKSF and Army High Threat CT EOD deployed in support of the police. Soldiers were seen in black Crye uniforms with MultiCam plate carriers, Ops Core SOTR respirator masks, and MSC SLAAP plates mounted to Ops Core helmets to defeat AK47 rounds. (Photo Metropolitan Police via Getty Images) the terrorists were watching at the time, they immediately surrendered. (The terrorists would later be found guilty of seven murders in all.)

On 5 May 1980 the SAS would draw thoroughly unwelcome world-wide attention with Operation 'Nimrod', the successful hostage rescue at the Iranian Embassy in central London. Six Iraqi-supported Iranian terrorists had seized the building and 26 hostages, including a uniformed police officer of the Diplomatic Protection Group, on 30 April. (Again, this operation has been covered extensively elsewhere, including in RAID 4, *Who Dares Wins: the SAS and the Iranian Embassy Siege 1980* by Gregory Fremont-Barnes and Pete Winner, so it only justifies the briefest overview here.) Control was handed to the SAS with the agreement of the Prime Minister and Home Secretary. After hostages were murdered B Squadron of 22 SAS, who were then on the Special Projects rotation, stormed the Embassy. Using diversions and distractions, the SAS breached into the building from multiple directions and conducted a largely textbook room-by-room clearance of the building, shooting dead all but one of the terrorists.

Today, UK Special Forces have a rotational system with both a primary and a secondary unit on-call for six months each as the national military CT or Special Projects team. This duty rotates between the SAS, SBS and the SFSG. As mentioned, however, the primary responsibility for terrorist incidents within the UK has always remained with the police, and the military are only called upon if the situation exceeds police capabilities.

The Metropolitan Police Force Firearms Unit has been at the forefront of the fight. Known by a variety of names during its 50-year history, the unit was first assigned a CT mandate as far back as 1975, although this was as a containment force while awaiting the arrival of the SAS. **SCO19**, as it is known today, is composed of four distinct elements, all of which may play their part during the response to a terrorist incident.

Typically, the first responders are three-officer Armed Response Vehicles (ARVs) with the radio callsign 'Trojan'. There are a number of these vehicles on the road around the clock to deal with all kinds of firearms calls. Alongside the ARVs is the Trojan Proactive Unit that provides armed support and advice for local forces. The Tactical Support Teams provide the next level of capability, including many tasks that were traditionally handled by the Specialist Firearms Officer teams. This includes support to CT operations and criminal hostage rescues. Finally there are the Counter-Terrorist Specialist Firearms Officers (CTSFOs), who are trained and equipped to UKSF standards. The CTSFO unit now provides the primary national CT intervention response, not the SAS or SBS. In 2016, following the attacks in Paris and Belgium, armed police levels were further strengthened, with 600 more officers to be recruited into armed roles under Operation 'Hercules'. Additionally, armed units across the UK have been integrated into a national response plan that provides coverage throughout the country, with even smaller regional teams training to deal with terrorist scenarios.

THE ATLAS NETWORK

Named after the Titan of Greek legend, ATLAS is a network of more than 30 CT units from 27 European Union members plus two non-EU countries (Norway and Switzerland). The organization was officially founded in the aftermath of the '9/11' attacks of September 2001, but informal links had been established as far back as 1996 – indeed, GSG9 had been sponsoring such contacts since the 1970s. Not surprisingly, some of the older and most experienced units like DSU, GSG9 and GIGN took the lead in establishing ATLAS. The units currently involved are:

EKO Cobra (Austria), DSU (Belgium), SUCT (Bulgaria), EAO (Cyprus), URNA (Czech Republic), AKS (Denmark), K Command (Estonia), Karhu (Finland), GIGN and RAID (France), GSG9 and SEK Baden Württemberg (Germany), EKAM (Greece), ERU (Ireland), TEK (Hungary), GIS and NOCS (Italy), OMEGA (Latvia), Aras (Lithuania), USP (Luxembourg), SAG (Malta), DSI (Netherlands), Beredskapstroppen/Delta (Norway), BOA (Poland), GOE (Portugal), Acvila and SIIAS (Romania), Lynx (Slovakia), Red Panther (Slovenia), GEO and UEI (Spain), NI (Sweden), Einsatzgruppe Tigris (Switzerland), and SCO19 (UK).

Each country is allowed membership of two units, typically one from the police and one from the military or national gendarmerie. Member units are assigned to develop specific subject areas based on their expertise. For instance, RAID are the lead unit for 'tubular' assaults on overground trains and buses, while GSG9 focus on MCT, GIGN on hijacked airliners, SCO19 on assaults on underground trains, and EKO Cobra on storming buildings, while DSU chaired the organization itself. ATLAS partner units also conduct joint exercises, and share intelligence and R&D findings.

Operation 'Octopus' in 2007 saw the Belgian DSU, Danish AKS, German GSG9, Swedish NI and Spanish GEO conduct a joint exercise against a scenario involving a hijacked ferry that crossed a number of jurisdictions.

A GSG9 team pictured at their base at St Augustin, Germany during an ATLAS exercise in 2007. Note their titanium Ulbrichts AM-95 helmets with ballistic visors. They carry the 5.56mm G36C fitted with EOTech optics, except for one officer with the G36K with underslung AG36 grenade launcher. (Photo Juergen Schwartz/Getty Images)

Austrian officers from EKO Cobra during an ATLAS exercise in 2007; note the optional upper arm protectors attached to their body armour. Surprisingly, along with LLM01 combined lasers and lights their 5.56mm Steyr AUG assault rifles still mount the integrated 1.5x magnification factory optic rather than the aftermarket Aimpoint or ACOG. (Photo Juergen Schwartz/ Getty Images)

Similar exercises have been held involving multiple simultaneous incidents, including hijacked aircraft; these are known as the ATLAS Common Challenge. In 2013, for instance, this was hosted in nine countries and involved operators from 36 units. GSG9's former commanding officer explained further in an interview:

'For example, in 2010 we trained [with] GIGN, the special unit of the French Gendarmerie, with two simultaneous entries on hijacked aircraft at Paris Orly airport; we practiced the liberation of ships with the Spaniards in 2011, and the protection of spectators during the World Cup. For 2013, we planned a Europe-wide large-scale exercise with ATLAS, [practicing] the reaction to large, simultaneous terror attacks on buildings, airplanes, trains and buses, with many hostages.'

GSG9 operator assigned to the German Embassy's close personal protection team in Baghdad, Iraq in 2009 discusses the merits of the G36C rifle with Australian soldiers. (Photo Cpl Rachel Ingram/courtesy Commonwealth of Australia)

As noted, prior to the formation of ATLAS an informal network for mutual assistance already existed. GSG9 hosted the first international CT workshop in 1979, and were instrumental in organizing and holding the first CTC or Combat Team Competition, which attracted 22 military and police units from across the globe. Now held every four years, the CTC typically lasts for five days and tests both the physical and mental strengths of a unit. Today it attracts more than 40 units (in 2005 including, for the first time, the Russian Alfa). GSG9 and the German SEKs tend to perform consistently well, as do the Swiss units such as Argus.

WEAPONS

In the immediate aftermath of Munich, fledgling European intervention units employed a range of issue and off-the-shelf kit. Units wore standard uniforms or green coveralls, and when helmets were worn they were often standard parachuting models. Weapons were often revolvers, selected due to their reliability, and 'long guns' were often whatever the parent organization had available. The SAS and GSG9 were amongst the first to realize that specialist weapons and equipment were required.

Scientists at the UK's defence research establishment at Porton Down invented a number of items that would revolutionize CT interventions. These included the first frangible 9mm ammunition, designed to expand within a shot terrorist's body and not overpenetrate to potentially harm hostages, and the first examples of the 'stun grenade' or 'flashbang'. This magnesium-based munition was developed to partially blind and deafen terrorists enclosed in a room for up to 5 seconds.

Handguns
The initial use of revolvers by a number of units pointed to the fact that in the 1970s little in the way of hollowpoint ammunition was being produced in the standard military semi-automatic pistol calibre of 9mm. For instance, the SAS carried standard ball ammunition in their MP5s during Operation 'Nimrod'. Revolver calibres were favoured by US law enforcement and competitive shooters, so a wide range of ammunition types including

Photographed in about 2006, this GIGN operator aims a 9mm Glock 17 mounting a Streamlight M3 light, and also carries a .357 Magnum Manurhin MR73 revolver holstered on his torso. (Photo Jack Guez/AFP/Getty Images)

hollowpoints were already available. GSG9 initially equipped with Smith & Wesson .38 and .357 Magnum revolvers, a move mirrored by GIGN with their Manurhin MR73. During Operation 'Fire Magic' the GSG9 commander Ulrich Wegener carried a 4in-barrel S&W Model 19 (which now resides in Bonn's Haus der Geschichte museum), whilst many of his men used the snub-nosed S&W Model 66 or the 9mm H&K P9S.

Gradually 9mm semi-automatics gained ground as more and more units appreciated the advantages of their larger magazine capacities, particularly as hollowpoint and frangible ammunition became more widely available. The SIG P220 and later P225 and P226 series were used, as was the Heckler & Koch P7 (PSP) 'squeeze-cocker', which GSG9 adopted after the Mogadishu operation. The British SAS retained their Browning High Powers until the late 1980s, when they were replaced with the P226.

Today the semi-automatic 9mm pistol reigns supreme. The Austrian Glock is by far the most widely employed; in fact, it is becoming unusual to see anything else in use. The Glock 17 with a Surefire tactical light is most common, with the compact

This GIGN officer wears full CBRN/HAZMAT protective equipment, complete with its own air supply. His weapon is the Fabrique National 5.7mm P90 fitted with an Aimpoint optic. (Photo Jack Guez/AFP/Getty Images)

Glock 19 also earning significant approval – including with the SAS, who have retired their P226s in its favour. The Belgians have even traded in their Fabrique Nationale Brownings for the Austrian pistol. Despite the MR73 still being their official issue, the Glock has also made inroads within GIGN.

Sub-machine guns & carbines

Units choose the Glock for one reason: its phenomenal reliability. For the same reason, European units adopted the Heckler & Koch MP5 series of sub-machine guns. In the early days most units used a range of Israeli Uzi, American Ingram, German Walther and Italian Beretta SMGs, but everything changed with GSG9's adoption of the MP5 in 1977. The SAS soon adopted

H **SPECIALIST EQUIPMENT EMPLOYED BY INTERVENTION UNITS**

(1) The AirTEP extraction platform, made on the 'umbrella' principle, can be underslung from a helicopter for the extraction of a hostage rescue team. With safety straps attached to the central suspension mast, and a floor of Kevlar web netting spread by five hinged metal struts, it can accommodate up to ten people.

(2) Chevrolet Suburban SWATEC truck mounting the Height Adjustable Rescue Assault System (HARAS), carrying an

assault team on the two-part fold-out platform.

(3) This kneeling operator with a hand-held tablet controls a six-wheel miniature Unmanned Ground Vehicle (UGV) as it speeds forward to carry out reconnaissance.

(4) This GIGN officer, armed with a Heckler & Koch MP7A1 and carrying a four-wheel UGV on his backpack, is deploying an extendable camera pole feeding to a view screen to look around corners or into windows.

(5) This small UAV (drone), also controlled by hand-held tablet, is fitted with low-light cameras and audio sensors.

this weapon, and before long virtually every intervention unit in Europe followed suit. Even units within the Eastern Bloc tried to get themselves black-market MP5s.

While the MP5 remains the primary assault weapon of the majority of European CT units, a range of 5.56mm carbine-length assault rifles are steadily gaining ground. They offer greater ballistic lethality and range in a similarly sized package, and 5.56mm is also seen as a more effective counter to terrorist use of body armour than 9mm. The 4.6mm MP7 from Heckler & Koch has seen some adoption including by GIGN's close-protection operators. Equally, the integrally suppressed (silenced) MP5SD remains popular in many teams, since its low sound signature has until very recently never been matched. The bullpup 5.7mm Fabrique Nationale P90 is used by units including the DSU, GEO, SIPA, GIGN and URNA, again particularly when fitted with a suppressor. Controversy around the ballistic effectiveness of its tiny bullet has dogged the weapon, but its compact size and low recoil are appreciated by teams operating in restrictive environments like aircraft and ships. It is often employed by lead scouts and those covering the shield-man.

Italian GIS operators display a range of weapons used by the unit; visible are the 5.56mm HK416 and Bushmaster M4 assault rifles, the 12-gauge Benelli M3 shotgun, the 5.56mm Minimi LMG, and a range of pistols. (Photo Laura Lezza/Getty Images)

Assault & battle rifles

Broadly, three types of assault rifle are employed by European units: the SIG 551/552/553 series, the Heckler & Koch G36 series, and various incarnations of the American-designed M4 carbine. The SIG SWAT and Commando 551 and 552 assault rifles have seen much use, principally with French, German and Spanish units. Their side-folding stocks make the SIG designs particularly compact, proving useful for divers and parachutists in particular. The British SCO19 have recently adopted two of the latest additions to the line of SIG assault rifles, the SG516 and the MCX.

The G36 is offered in a bewildering number of variants based on three key types: the standard full-length G36, the compact G36K, and the even shorter G36C, often seen with a side-folding stock. The G36 family are certainly the most common assault rifle employed by European units, although there is little commonality in exact specification. In France, for example, RAID and BRI-BAC use the G36C with a selector group allowing only single shots and two-round bursts, while GIGN typically carry the KA3 variant which offers fully selective fire. GSG9 tend to carry the G36C in a number of configurations, often with a suppressor.

The M4 design and later evolutions like the HK416 are also widely employed. Norwegian Delta use the Colt Canada C8 SFW, a model employed by the SAS as the L119A1 until their recent adoption of the improved L119A2. The Italian NOCS issue

Members of a Sonder Einsatztrupp (SET) from GSG9 photographed in the mid 1980s with an impressive display of their weapons and equipment. Visible under magnification are 7.62mm PSG-1 and Mauser SP66 sniper rifles; 9mm MP5A3, MP5K and MP5SD3 sub-machine guns; the 12-gauge HK502 shotgun; and a range of .357 Magnum revolvers and 9mm P7 PSP pistols. (Photographer unknown; private collection)

Bushmaster M4 carbines, as did GROM until their adoption of the HK416. In fact, if any one weapon looks likely to eclipse all others it is the HK416, another product-improved version of the M4.

However, some units do use other platforms. The Belgians issue the Mk16 SCAR, while until recently the GIS used the HK53 carbine, essentially a 5.56mm version of the MP5. GIGN still maintain a number of bullpup FAMAS G2 assault rifles fitted with Picatinny rail systems; these are not generally favoured as assault weapons, but have a useful ability to launch both offensive and defensive rifle grenades. The other bullpups typically encountered are the Austrian Steyr AUG, used predictably enough by EKO Cobra in its carbine-length option, and the FN2000 employed by the Spanish GEO. Indeed, some units use a mix of assault rifles. GIGN has been seen in recent years with the Mk16, FAMAS G2, HK416 and SIG 552 rifles. Others prefer a single design: witness GSG9's long relationship with the G36 series, only recently eclipsed by the introduction of the HK416. The long guns of European intervention units often feature an unusual stock, a result of the extensive use of ballistic visors on helmets. Standard stocks often impede the use of weapon sights, so a modified stock is fitted. Swiss manufacturer Brugger & Thomet (B&T), joined recently by Heckler & Koch, produce many of these aftermarket stocks, canted to an angle of 45 degrees to help address this particular challenge.

Battle rifles have always had a place in European intervention units' armouries, and none more so than the iconic Heckler & Koch G3, which has been popular since the 1970s. Firing the 7.62mm round, it has often been deployed with an optic and bipod as a sniper or marksman rifle. Today's versions, carried by the likes of GSG9 and DSU, feature aftermarket rails and adjustable stocks. SCO19 has purchased a unique scoped, short-barrelled G3K modified with the stock and pistol grip from the H&K MSG90 sniper rifle. Recently the G3 has been at least partly overtaken by the 7.62mm HK417, and indeed there has even been some movement towards the use of HK417s by assaulters; for instance, the Spanish GEO have purchased a number of 12in-barrel versions for this

A sniper from GSG9 taking aim through the Schmidt & Bender PMII scope on his 7.62mm HK417 marksman rifle. An Aimpoint Micro T1 red-dot optic is mounted above the telescopic sight for emergency close-range shooting. (Photo courtesy Bundespolizei/GSG9)

purpose. It is more widely deployed as a marksman or spotter's rifle, and units as disparate as BRI-BAC and URNA now employ the HK417 in this manner.

Sniper rifles

In terms of dedicated sniper rifles, European designs have always found favour. Perhaps the most widely used until recent times was the 7.62mm Heckler & Koch PSG-1, a somewhat delicate but superbly accurate rifle. Although still more than a match for younger designs, the PSG-1 has been replaced by more recent types like the HK417 in its sniper configuration. Intriguingly, the Russian Alfa Group use a limited number of the civilian version of the HK417, the MR762 (they also use M4-pattern carbines and Glock pistols).

The bolt-action 7.62mm Mauser SP66 once equipped the majority of European units, but it has been largely superseded by designs from the British firm of Accuracy International, a company that began life supplying sniper rifles to the SAS and SBS. Their AWS or Arctic Warfare Suppressed (known as the G25 in German service) is a folding-stock, integrally suppressed 7.62mm design that was heavily adopted, as were its non-suppressed versions, the AW and PM. GIGN used hand-built versions of the 7.5mm FR-F1 and later 7.62mm F2 before these were replaced in 2003 by the Accuracy International PM and the Tikka T3 Tactical in 7.62mm, and the Accuracy International AW Magnum in .338 Lapua Magnum. Along with the Accuracy International, bolt-action designs from Sako have also proved popular; the Sako TRG 22 and TRG 42 in 7.62mm and .338 respectively are in common use by Polish, Danish and Norwegian snipers.

Indeed, following a military trend, there has been a distinct move towards heavier-calibre sniper rifles by intervention units, even though they will be used at much shorter ranges than their regular military counterparts. These are typically bolt-action designs in .300 Winchester Magnum or .338 Lapua Magnum. Intervention unit sniper teams will often be composed of a sniper with a bolt-action rifle for accuracy, and a spotter with a semi-automatic platform to provide fast follow-up shots or covering fire. The bolt-action Steyr SSG08 in a range of calibres, including 7.62mm and .338 Lapua Magnum, is a very recent design developed in close cooperation with EKO Cobra; it edged out competition from the Accuracy International AXMC in .338, which has since been adopted by the Belgian DSU. The Swiss Scorpion unit and GSG9 both employ the bolt-action French PGM Mini Hecate in the same calibre.

The .50cal anti-matériel rifle is still deployed for specific purposes. The weapon was used during the Saint-Denis operation by RAID to try to punch through the outer brick walls of the target apartment. The .50 PGM Hecate in a number of configurations is popular with EKO Cobra, GIGN and GSG9, although nearly all keep at least one or two examples of the semi-automatic Barrett M82A1 in their armouries.

Miscellaneous weapons

Most units also have a number of light machine guns available for large-scale incidents requiring suppressive fire; GIGN deployed at least one Minimi Para during the Dammartin-en-Goële incident. RAID maintains a number of 5.56mm Minimi and 7.62mm Maximi LMGs following their experiences during the infamous Gang de Roubaix operation, while GSG9 use the magazine-fed 7.62mm Heckler & Koch G8A1. A number of former Eastern Bloc units, including the Polish BOA, still use the excellent belt-fed PKM medium machine gun.

At the other end of the lethality spectrum, intervention teams also use a number of less-than-lethal technologies, from the common OC or pepper spray and X-26 Tasers to handheld water cannons, and both 12-gauge and 40mm 'beanbag' rounds. A DSU commander explained that he prefers his men to take terrorists alive for interrogation if at all possible. 'We preferably shoot them in the leg, arm or shoulder. If possible we use the FN 303, a weapon that fires a less lethal munition which hurts and stops a perpetrator.'[1] The FN 303 is gaining wide acceptance as a less-than-lethal option; a compressed-air launcher, it fires a range of .68in 'paintball'-style projectiles that deliver 'a sufficiently dissuasive level of pain within the projectile's impact zone to

An excellent example of the use of UAVs by intervention units. Here a member of the French BRI-BAC controls one (hovering, mid-left) during a 2016 exercise on the Paris Metro network – see also Plate H5. (Photo Miguel Medina/AFP/Getty Images)

disable targets', according to its manufacturer Fabrique Nationale. Rounds incorporating OC irritants are also available. A similar weapon is the French Verney Carron Flash-Ball double-barrel launcher, which fires a proprietary 44mm rubber ball projectile.

Shotguns have always remained a more unusual sight in European hands, although all units employ specialist shortened weapons for breaching or to deliver Ferret CS gas projectiles. The most popular remains the dependable Remington 870, a pump-action design that is often shortened to a pistol-grip configuration for use in ballistic breaching. The Benelli M3 and M4 series of semi-pump shotguns are also widely employed. More unusual designs occasionally encountered include the Russian Molot Vepr and the Saiga 12 used by the BRI-BAC and RAID. Resembling Kalashnikov designs, these are actually semi-automatic shotguns fed from an AK-like curved magazine. Italian units have employed the Franchi line of combat shotguns, including the famous SPAS-12 and the magazine-fed SPAS-15. GSG9 perhaps pioneered the use of combat shotguns with the HK502, one of which was issued to each GSG9 SET during the 1970s and early 1980s.

Some 40mm grenade launchers are employed to fire impact-fused flashbangs, CS gas and chemical smoke in support of assaults. If necessary, high explosive grenades can also be used; images from the RAID operation at Saint-Denis show the impacts of 40mm rounds (probably military High Explosive Dual Purpose) in the external wall of the apartment. GEO, GIGN and RAID use the South African-designed Milkor multi-shot launcher, while GSG9 maintain stocks of the HK69A1 standalone launcher along with the underslung AG36 and M320. The B&T GL06 is also seeing increasing use by EKO Cobra and others.

9 January 2015: GIGN storming the Dammartin-en-Goële print works. This photo was actually taken as the perpetrators of the *Charlie Hebdo* murders were exiting the building in a storm of gunfire. The officers in the background are dismounting from an SUV while at right a Renault Sherpa 4x4 light APC speeds forward carrying the assault team. The on-board ramp has been raised to facilitate entry to the upper floor of the print works. (Photo © Gendarmerie Nationale/F. Balsamo)

SELECT BIBLIOGRAPHY

Andre, Dom, *Flashbang Magazine*, various issues (Paris; Nimrod)

Andre, Dom, *Special Units* (Paris; Nimrod, 2016)

Fremont-Barnes, Gregory & Pete Winner, *Who Dares Wins: the SAS and the Iranian Embassy Siege 1980* (Oxford; Osprey, 2009)

Katz, Samuel M., *Global Counterstrike: International Counterterrorism* (Lerner Publications, 2004)

Katz ,Samuel M., *The Illustrated Guide to the World's Top Counter-Terrorist Forces* (Hong Kong; Concord, 1995)

McNab, Chris, *Storming Flight 181: GSG 9 and the Mogadishu Hijack* (Oxford; Osprey, 2011)

Smith, Stephen, *Stop! Armed Police! Inside the Met's Firearms Unit* (London; Robert Hale Ltd, 2013)

Thompson, Leroy, *The Rescuers: The World's Top Anti-Terrorist Units* (Boulder; Paladin Press, 1986)

Tophoven, Rolf & Verlag Bernard & Graefe, *GSG9: German Response to Terrorism* (Berlin; Monch, 1985)

various, *Kommando Magazine* (Nurernberg; SJ Publications)

various, *Special Ops: Journal of the Elite Forces & SWAT Units* (Hong Kong; Concord)

Online source notes (superior reference numbers in text):

(1) https://www.rt.com/news/354068-gsg9-paris-attacks-terrorism/

(2) http://www.special-ops.org/news/special-forces/dsu-belgium-determined-hunt-terrorists/amp/

(3) http://www.20minutes.fr/planete/1521567-20150120-dammartin-goele-chiens-gign-portaient-gilets-pare-balles

(4) http://www.leparisien.fr/charlie-hebdo/un-policier-du-raid-raconte-l-assaut-de-l-hyper-cacher-02-04-2015 4659233.php

(5) http://www.telegraph.co.uk/news/worldnews/europe/france/12003186

(6) http://www.gign.org/groupe-intervention/?page_id=407

(7) http://corpidelite.net/afm/2012/05/intervista-ad-ulrich-k-wegener/

(8) https://www.merkur.de/bayern/9-beamter-befreiten-landshut-2552919.html

GLOSSARY OF ABBREVIATIONS

ACOG	Advanced Combat Optical Gunsight (Trijicon magnified rifle optic)
AirTEP	Airborne Tactical Extraction Platform
AKS	Special Intervention Unit (Danish national intervention unit)
APC	armoured personnel carrier
ARV	Armed Response Vehicle (see SCO19)
B&T	Brugger & Thomet
BBE	Bijzondere Bijstands Eeinheid (Dutch national intervention unit)
BFE+	Beweissicherungs und Festnahmeeinheit Plus (German police tactical support unit)
BOA	Biuro Operacji Antyterrorystycznych (Polish police intervention unit)
BRI-BAC	Brigades de Recherché et d'Intervention – Brigade Anti-Commando (Paris police intervention unit)
BSIJ	Brigada Specială de Intervenţie a Jandarmeriei (Romanian police tactical unit)
CAD	combat assault dog
CBRN	chemical, biological, radiological, and nuclear
CGSU	General Commissariat Special Unit (see ESI and DSU)
CQB	close-quarter battle
CRW	counter-revolutionary warfare
CS	'tear gas'
CT	counter-terrorist
CTC	Combat Team Competition (GSG9)
CTSFO	Counter Terrorist Specialist Firearms Officer (London Metropolitan Police intervention unit)
Daesh	See IS
DMR	Designated Marksman Rifle (scoped semi-automatic sniper rifle)
DSI	Dienst Speciale Interventies (Dutch CT organization)
DSU	Directorate of Special Units (Belgian CT organization)
EDD	explosive-detection dog
EKAM	Eidikes Katastaltikes Antitromokratikes Monades (Greek national intervention unit)
EKO	Einsatzkommando ('action unit')
EMOE	explosive method of entry
EOD	explosive ordnance disposal ('bomb disposal')
ERU	Emergency Response Unit (Irish police intervention unit)
ESI	Escadron Special d'Intervention (Belgian police intervention unit)
ETA	Euskadi Ta Askatasuna (Basque terrorist organization)
FAO	Force Operational Support (of GIGN)
FN	Fabrique Nationale
FOR	Force Observation Research (of GIGN)
FSK	Forsvarets Spesialkommando (Norwegian SOF)
FSP	Force Security Protection (of GIGN)
GIA	Armed Islamic Group (Algerian terrorist organization)
GIGN	Groupe d'Intervention de la Gendarmerie Nationale (French Gendarmerie national intervention unit)
GIPN	Groupes d'Intervention de la Police Nationale (former French police intervention units)
GIS	Gruppo di Intervento Speciale (Italian military intervention unit)
GK	Gendarmeriekommando
GOE	Grupo de Operações Especiais (Portuguese national intervention unit)
GEO	Grupos de Operaciones Especiales (Spanish police intervention unit)
GROM	Grupa Reagowania Operacyjno Manewrowego (Polish Army SOF)
GSG9	Grenzschutzgruppe 9 (German Border Police intervention unit)
HAHO	high altitude high opening (parachuting technique)
HALO	high altitude low opening (parachuting technique)
HARAS	Height Adjustable Rescue Assault System (vehicle-mounted ramp)
HK/ H&K	Heckler & Koch

HMMWV	High Mobility Multipurpose Wheeled Vehicle ('Humvee', 'Hummer')
IED	improvised explosive device
IS	'Islamic State' or Daesh (Middle Eastern Islamic extremist terrorist movement)
JRA	Japanese Red Army (Japanese terrorist organization)
KSK	Kommando Spezialkräfte (German Army SOF)
LMG	light machine gun
MCT	Maritime Counter Terrorist
MEK	Mobile Einsatzkommanden (Austrian tactical unit)
MJK	Marinejegerkommandoen (Norwegian SOF)
MOE	method of entry
MTFA	marauding terrorist firearms attack (type of terrorist attack)
MVD	Ministerstvo Vnutrennikh Del / Ministry of Internal Affairs (Russian internal security)
NOCS	Nucleo Operativo Centrale di Sicurezza (Italian police intervention unit)
OAG	Operational Action Group (see GEO)
OMON	Otryad Mobilny Osobogo Naznacheniya / Special Purpose Mobility Unit (Russian Federal Police intervention unit)
OPEC	Organization of the Petroleum Exporting Countries
PFLP	Popular Front for the Liberation of Palestine (Palestinian terrorist organization)
PI2G	Peloton d'intervention interrégional de Gendarmerie (former French regional tactical units)
PIRA	Provisional Irish Republican Army (Irish terrorist organization)
PKM	Pulemyot Kalashnikova (Russian-designed medium machine gun)
POSA	Protection Observation Support and Arrest (Belgian police tactical units)
QRF	quick reaction force (fast response back-up unit)
RAF	Red Army Faction (German terrorist organization)
RAID	Research Assistance Intervention Dissuasion (French police intervention unit)
RPG	rocket-propelled grenade (Russian-designed rocket launcher)
SAJ	Specijalna Antiteroristicka Jedinica (Serbian national intervention unit)
SAS	Special Air Service (British Army SOF)
SBS	Special Boat Service (British Royal Navy SOF)
SCO19	Specialist Command 19 (London Metropolitan Police firearms unit)
SEG	Special Einsatzgruppen (Austrian tactical unit)
SET	Sonder Einsatztrupp (see GSG9)
SFSG	Special Forces Support Group (British Army SOF)
SIE	Special Interventie Eskadron (see ESI)
SIIAS	Serviciul Independent de Interventii si Actiuni Speciale (Romanian police intervention unit)
SIPA	State Investigation and Protection Agency (Bosnia-Herzegovina)
SMG	sub-machine gun
SOF	Special Operations Forces
SP	Special Projects (see SAS)
SPAP	Samodzielny Pododdział Antyterrorystyczny Policji (Polish police regional tactical units)
SSU	Special Support Unit (Bosnia-Herzegovina police intervention unit)
SWAT	special weapons and tactics
TEK	Counter Terrorism Centre (Hungarian)
UAV	unmanned aerial vehicle ('drone')
UGV	unmanned ground vehicle ('droid')
UIM	Unit Interventie Mariniers (see BBE)
UKSF	United Kingdom Special Forces (British military SOF)
UOU	Útvar Osobitného Určenia (Slovakian police intervention unit)
URNA	Útvar Rychlého Nasazení (Czech national intervention unit)
VSS	Vintovka Snayperskaya Spetsialnaya (Russian-designed Vintorez suppressed rifle)
WEGA	Wiener Einsatzgruppe Alarmabteilung (Viennese police intervention unit)
ZJ	Zasahova Jednotka (Czech police tactical unit)

INDEX

Note: page numbers in bold refer to illustrations, captions and plates.